BUYING PROPER
(third ᴇ

BUYING PROPERTY IN PORTUGAL
(third edition)

GABRIELLE COLLISON

First Published in Great Britain 2007
by Bookshaker

Second Edition Published in Great Britain 2011
by Summertime Publishing

Third Edition Published in Great Britain 2015
by Gabrielle Lea Publishing

A CIP catalogue record for this book is available
from the British Library.

ISBN: 978-0-9572186-4-2

Cover photograph by Mark Sparrow

Cover design by Andrew Pendlebury
www.perfectdesignbits.com

For Roy and Jim.

Praise For This Book

Another indispensable guide to buying property in Portugal by Gabrielle Collison. Don't even think about moving to Portugal without it!

Simon Pownall
Owner of www.expatsportugal.com

Buying a property abroad can be a daunting task if you don't know the law and custom of the country you're buying in. We've all heard horror stories of how people have lost money or even their homes when not taking sufficient care when buying a home overseas. If Portugal is a country that takes your fancy then Gabrielle's latest edition of her guide to buying a property in Portugal can take those fears away. Everything you need to know about the Portuguese property market, the legal process and the pitfalls to watch out for, are set out in this invaluable guide. If you only buy one book on buying a property in Portugal, make sure it is this one. It's the first and last word on the subject.

Mark Sparrow
Journalist, broadcaster, columnist & photographer
@markgsparrow
www.about.me/marksparrow

Property buyers in Portugal, say Olá to your new bible. I certainly wish I'd been able to consult such a nuts-and-bolts guide to purchasing a Spanish property before we made the move over here in 2004. For the Iberian property market is one quagmire that's difficult to avoid getting bogged down in. This is the third edition, so why buy it? This is unquestionably an idiot's guide to investing in a property in Portugal. Everything is covered, from regions, location and type of property to agents, builders and legal documentation. If you only buy two books before your move to Portugal, make sure this is one. The other? An English-Portuguese dictionary. Collison, true to form, covers the importance of learning the lingo before your relocation. Entertaining case studies from those who have made their home in Portugal bring a bit of light relief to a textbook lesson in how to buy a Portuguese property.

Matthew Hirtes
Author
Going Local in Gran Canaria
www.grancanarialocal.com

Buy this book if you want to avoid the pitfalls of buying a property in Portugal. You will save yourself loads of hassle and money and find a property that matches your needs if you follow Gabrielle's advice.

Not only are there case studies to help you understand both the benefits and drawbacks, there are step-by-step guides to the buying process, a detailed description of the property market in each area of Portugal, help on choosing representation or buying privately, a section on managing builders and avoiding planning problems, and a hugely useful guide to the legal process. This book has everything you need, and most importantly, Gabrielle isn't trying to sell you anything, you're getting straightforward, honest advice that you know you can trust! Go on, realise your dreams in Portugal!

Debbie Jenkins
Author
Going Native in Murcia
www.nativespain.com

Moving home is stressful. Throw in a foreign country, an unfamiliar language, different laws and customs and even the most desirable property can become the stuff of nightmares. So when I started my searches in Portugal it was a blessed relief to find a book that simply 'told it like it is'. With simple checklists supported by more detailed explanations, the pros and cons of various options laid out in an easy-to-read manner and neither over-hyped nor forbidding. There is no one route to find the perfect 'place-in-the-sun' but this book will be a wise and trusty companion along your way.

Tim Serle

Regulations and laws change at a bewildering speed in Portugal and so an up-to-date book is essential. This one goes much further than others by explaining every step and the potential pitfalls. As well as suggesting that you check the qualifications of a stated professional and the status of a property, it tells you the department that holds that information, the relevant website to visit and then — and this is its genius — it guides the non-Portuguese reader on how to correctly use the site and gather information. You will be amazed at the volume of information you can extract once armed with this powerful book and careful reading will hopefully prevent many expensive mistakes being made.

I recommend it not only for its meticulous detail and practical advice, but because the writer obviously knows the people, the property world and the country very well indeed. It is written in an honest, unsentimental style and when I'd finished I felt I understood the nature of the place a little more.

Kim Thomas

A comprehensive and accessible guide to moving to Portugal. The book strikes a balance between realism and the desire for a change of scenery, and covers a range of subjects including finding a property, learning the language, and sorting out the financial aspects of moving to a new country. There are also several useful case studies, which bring a personal perspective to the guide, as well as lists of the pros and cons of the various options available when deciding where to live, what kind of property to buy and whether to make the move.

Scar de Courcier
Senior Editor
Expat Focus
www.expatfocus.com

Acknowledgements

I'd like to thank Cláudia Silva of Chavetejo Mediação Imobiliária Lda (real estate agency) - *www.chavetejo.com* for her help and input regarding the central region of Portugal, Mark Sparrow - *www.about.me/marksparrow* for supplying the cover photograph, Andrew Pendlebury - *www.perfectdesignbits.com* for the cover design and all those who contributed short stories about their move to Portugal.

Contents

Introduction   1

Caveat Emptor – Let The Buyer Beware   5

Relocating   9
     Learning Portuguese   16
        CASE STUDY: LUCY PEPPER   *21*

The Buying Process At-a-Glance   25

Off-Plan, New Build, Resale or Self-Build   29
     Off-Plan   29
     New Build   31
     Resale   32
     Self-Build   33

Location   35
     Countryside   36
     Villages   37
     Coast   38
     Towns & Cities   39
        CASE STUDY: EMMA CRABTREE   *40*

Regions of Portugal   45
     North   46
     Centre   52
     Lisbon   57
     Alentejo   63
     Algarve   68
        CASE STUDY: EMMA BRUNTON   *74*

Real Estate Agents and Vendors   81
     Checking Out Portuguese Agents   82
     Checking Out UK Agents   84
     Checking Out Private Vendors   86
     Other Checks You Should Carry Out   87

CASE STUDY: MANDY DE AZEVEDO COUTINHO 93

Builders and Architects **99**
Checking Out Your Builder 99
Checking Out Your Architect 102
Planning Procedure 103
Recommendations 106
Translation and Supervision 107
Buying From a Builder and Building Contracts 107
Paying Builders and Architects 110
Builders and Legal Advice 111
CASE STUDY: HAZEL DICKSON 112

Professional Legal Advice **115**
Types of Representative 115
Doing Your Own Checks 118
Selecting Your Legal Representative 118
What You Should Expect 119
Promissory Contract 121
Power of Attorney 123
Final Deed 124
What You Should Receive 127
Complaints 128
CASE STUDY: ANDREW PENDLEBURY 129

Mortgages and Offshore Buyers **135**

What's What **141**
Land Registry – Conservatória do Registo Predial 141
Notary — Cartório Notarial 144
Casa Pronta 147
Tax Office — Serviço das Finanças 148
Habitation Licence, Pre-1951 Certificate and Ficha Técnica de
Habitação 154
Utilities 156
Energy Efficiency Certificate 165
Swimming Pool Licences 167
Maps 168
CASE STUDY: DONNA & PETER NUTTER 170

Condominiums   **175**

Summary: Top Ten Buying Tips   **179**

Selling a Property   **181**

Renting   **189**
  Long-Term Rental   190
  Holiday Rental   194
    CASE STUDY: DAVID HINMAN   *199*

Residency   **203**
  Visits   203
  Residency Certificate   203
  Residency Card   204
  Immigration Office — Serviço de Estrangeiros e Fronteiras (SEF)

                                                                  205
  Non-EU Citizens   206
  Golden Visa   207
  Tax   208
    CASE STUDY: BEN TAYLOR   *212*

About Gabrielle   **217**

Appendices   **219**
  IMT (Purchase Tax) 2015   219
  Property Purchase Checklist   221
  Purchase Budget Calculator   225

Introduction

If you're thinking of buying a property in Portugal and want to get things right first time – then this straightforward little guide has been written for you.

But why should you take my advice and how does this book differ from all the other stuff you could read? Well to find out, read on...

My family bought a property in the Algarve in 2000, which inevitably meant that I began spending more and more time in Portugal.

Due to the fact that I love learning languages and had already learnt Spanish, French and some Italian, I picked up a working knowledge of Portuguese fairly quickly.

On hearing that I was conversant in the language, many non-Portuguese-speaking friends and acquaintances started asking me to do them small favours.

While doing these favours, I visited more than my fair share of local government departments, authorities, utility companies and businesses to sort out various problems, in particular those surrounding property purchases.

I soon began to realise that a fair number of the people I was helping had been caught out by their lack of knowledge of the bureaucracy, and their unfamiliarity with the language. Several of them had also been far too trusting and naïve.

The property world is naturally a cutthroat one and while many purchases go through smoothly, there are others that could only be described as 'nightmares'!

Little by little, I learnt all about property documents and the processes involved in buying a property in Portugal, and I started to write about the potential pitfalls on various Internet forums.

My reputation for being fairly knowledgeable soon spread and other people started to contact me for help and advice. I was also invited to appear on Kiss FM's *Straight Talk with Phill Gilbert*, a phone-in radio show in the Algarve, and later asked to assist with the filming of a TV programme about relocating to Portugal.

Writing a book therefore seemed the logical next step and provides me with a way to help even more people navigate the Portuguese property market.

This is the third edition and I hope it is even more comprehensive than the first two.

Now, I will warn you — this book is not your typical 'buying abroad' book. It isn't written to encourage you to buy a place in Portugal. If you're already keen on Portugal then you don't need me to persuade you —

you just need to know what you have to do next and how to get things right.

There are many other books out there giving general property information and travel advice on Portugal but my aim is to give specific, and hopefully more streetwise, advice that might just save you a lot of time and a little money in the process.

This book will help you get your thinking cap on about buying a property in Portugal and the things you should check for yourself, whether you decide to use legal representation or not.

While I'm on the subject of legal representation, let me just make something clear — this book is not in any way advising you to shun legal advice and 'go it alone' when buying property in Portugal. Unfortunately, mistakes can still be made despite doing exhaustive checks and searches. However, by using reputable, independent legal advice, alongside doing your own thorough checks, this will no doubt lessen your chances of running into problems.

It should also be noted that changes in this area are frequent, and while I have endeavoured to make this book as accurate and as up to date as possible, some laws and websites may still have changed since publication.

Likewise, different areas and regions in Portugal often interpret the laws and regulations in their own unique way and this can sometimes lead to confusion when making general statements for the country as a whole.

The best advice in relation to buying a property in Portugal, or in any country in the world come to that, is that while respecting the local business culture, only do as you would be happy to do back home.

Do not worry about appearing difficult or demanding and do not feel embarrassed to keep asking as many questions as you wish. Buying a property is obviously a very expensive and potentially risky business.

If you do not take precautions and fail to investigate thoroughly, you could end up paying dearly further down the line.

I hope this book serves as a practical and reliable resource when buying property in Portugal and I wish you *boa sorte* (good luck)!

Gabrielle Collison

Caveat Emptor – Let The Buyer Beware

Up until forty years ago, Portugal was under a tightly controlled, fascist regime.

During the fascist era there was an atmosphere of fear. People kept things very much to themselves and families stuck closely together.

The government was seen as the enemy and the average person was frightened of officialdom.

Nepotism and cronyism were normal and sometimes, whole families controlled municipal councils and certain jobs. Corruption was rife with a heavy controlling bureaucracy.

Portugal has made great strides forward in recent years with the Internet having a huge impact on record keeping and reducing bureaucracy. However, be aware that old attitudes and ideas still linger, especially in more remote and rural locations, and seem to be only very slowly dying out.

The above factors, together with a history of rampant tax evasion, meant that Portugal was held back from competing with the rest of Europe and the recent global recession hit Portugal harder than most, resulting in a request to the EU-IMF for a €78 billion bailout in 2011 and the introduction of austerity measures, a cut on state spending and tax increases.

In May 2014, the Portuguese prime minister announced the official end of the country's three-year bailout. He did so by invoking *"the solemn duty of this and future governments to do everything in our power to ensure that history does not repeat itself"*.

There are signs that Portugal is finally emerging from the recession but things still remain fragile, and at the time of writing, unemployment continues to be high at 13.9% (source: Eurostat).

On the face of it, the Portuguese seem very welcoming, friendly and accommodating to foreigners and this is true to a large extent. They can also be very helpful, going out of their way to assist at times.

However, people are people and one must also bear in mind that many areas in Portugal only survive due to tourism and real estate. Therefore, a smiling, welcoming face may not always be genuine.

Both Portuguese and fellow nationals, who profess to be your good friend, may later on show themselves to be anything but and seemingly charming people may turn out to be nothing more than polished actors.

The lure of the Euro sign can be just too much for some people and if there is a chance to make money at your expense then it might well happen. This is a sad fact of life in any country, and Portugal is no exception, so don't let your guard down for one minute!

Never let anyone else, including 'professionals', take control of your life and your finances without first checking them out thoroughly and obtaining independent references. While very rare, there have been cases of 'professionals' absconding with people's money, so it is always best to 'err on the side of caution' when dealing with people.

Both Portuguese and expatriates will sometimes speak of doing things the 'old Portuguese way'. This usually refers to a more laid-back and casual method of buying property without using any legal advice (and trying to avoid paying as much tax as possible). It used to be the way for many years in Portugal.

However, I would not recommend this as an approach to buying property, especially for foreigners. If something was to go wrong, you could find yourself having all sorts of problems in the future. Please, be careful!

CAVEAT EMPTOR - LET THE BUYER BEWARE

Relocating

People on holiday can often be seen staring dreamily into real estate agents' windows.

When you're in a holiday mood with the sun shining and wine flowing, Portugal can seem like paradise. However, the worst thing you could possibly do during this holiday state of mind is to suddenly decide that Portugal is the place you want to live and start viewing properties and put a deposit down for one.

As with all big decisions in life, research is the key and one must always remember that *living* somewhere is completely different to *holidaying* there.

Even if you are just thinking in terms of a holiday home, a lot of careful consideration needs to be given, especially if you are going to need rental income to sustain your venture. More and more people have bought holiday homes over recent years, so competition can be fierce to get your property rented out.

You should do some thorough research on the likely income you will receive *after* you have paid for taxes, cleaning and laundry, condominium charges (if on a complex) and regular maintenance to the property.

Upkeeping a property to a decent standard can work out a lot more expensive than you might think!

Another thing to consider when buying a holiday home is the best location for holiday rentals and what type of clientele you want to attract. If you would like to have a remote, countryside location but the more popular rentals are on the livelier coast, then you may have to compromise a little.

Obviously the summer months will be the peak time for rentals and income and therefore you might only get to use your property during the colder, rainier months. Is this something that suits you or are you prepared to forgo some of your income?

If you are looking for an investment then you need to speak to independent, overseas financial consultants to see what the long-term and short-term capital growth opportunities are likely to be. What might suit one investor might not suit another, so it is imperative that you seek sound, qualified advice.

After more than three years of struggling house prices, Portugal's housing market now seems to be recovering. According to figures released by the *Instituto Nacional de Estatística – INE*, house prices increased by 4% in the first quarter, 5.9% in the second quarter and 4.9% in the third quarter of 2014 when compared to the same quarters in the previous year.

House transactions were also up in each quarter of 2014 compared to 2013.

However, it should be noted that while many cities and municipalities have experienced house price growth, others are still struggling.

Relocating on a permanent basis to another country, especially one which has a different language and culture, needs thorough planning. If you have children and need to work, this is even more crucial. Finding work in Portugal, if you do not speak fluent Portuguese, is not at all easy and even then you will find that many jobs only pay the minimum wage. In 2015 this is €589.20 a month.

Now, for those of you thinking that you will only be working amongst the expatriate community and that you will find plenty of work, with little need to learn Portuguese, please think again! Foreigners have been coming to live in Portugal, particularly the Algarve, for many years and a lot of potential business opportunities have become over-saturated.

You must also consider the fact that many Portuguese (and the increasing Eastern European population in Portugal) speak excellent English and can quite often offer the same services a lot cheaper.

Having enough money behind you to live for a minimum of one year without having to work, is a wise move and certainly important if you are trying out a business venture to see if it might work. You will really need some form of security behind you.

Those with businesses, which can be run from anywhere in the world via the Internet, or retirees with generous pensions, and/or alternative income and savings, generally survive the best in Portugal.

If you have children, what about schooling? Will you be sending your children to the local school or to a private, fee-paying, international school? If so, can you afford this? What age are your children and are they at a stage in their life where they will pick up the language and integrate easily? It is generally considered that before the age of seven is best.

So think carefully. You don't want to put your family through the misery and upheaval of relocating only to have to return through lack of research and doing something on a whim.

Ask yourself why you really want to relocate and what you hope to gain from it. Many people cite reasons, such as:

- ❑ Less crime.
- ❑ Better life for their children.
- ❑ Warmer climate.
- ❑ Less stress.
- ❑ Lower cost of living.
- ❑ Better standard of living.

However, do your research to see if those things are actually true in the area you are hoping to live. Often the reality is quite different from the perception.

While some of Portugal is lost in a time warp, and still rather old-fashioned, quiet and quaint, other parts (particularly the major cities) are like anywhere else in modern 21st-century Europe.

Also, if you are someone who gets impatient when waiting for more than two minutes in the post office to be served, then think long and hard about living in Portugal or you could end up more stressed out than ever! The Portuguese generally do things in their own good time and won't be hurried by you tapping your fingers on the counter, or tutting loudly.

In addition, Portuguese bureaucracy can have you wandering around in complete circles for hours, if not days and months on end. Read Portuguese newspapers and websites, and expatriate magazines and forums to get a feel for the country and its problems, as well as its obvious advantages.

Renting for an extended period of time is an excellent idea. This will give you the opportunity to look around the area you are thinking of relocating to as a native in order to make sure it is what you really want. It will also give you the opportunity to check out other areas around Portugal.

You could also consider renting out your home in the UK or other country of origin to see if Portugal is for you before selling up lock, stock and barrel. This way you will always have something to return to should the need arise.

Experiencing all the seasons is a must too. Hot, sunny Portugal can also be cold, wet and windy at times and remember that most houses do not have central heating and often get very damp.

Other things that you may wish to consider are:

❑ Is a coastal area, while nice in the winter, going to be too busy and noisy in the summer?

❑ Is a place that is lively and entertaining in the summer going to be too dead and dull in the winter?

❑ What are the local amenities and services on offer? What is the local transport like?

❑ Do you need a lot of social contact, or are you happy to live quite remote and isolated?

❑ Do you want or need the support of fellow nationals around you, or do you want to be a million miles away from the nearest expat?

Make a list of the things you really need and want and those you definitely don't. Being far away from the nearest shops and banks can seem bearable during a two-week holiday, but on a daily basis it may become extremely irritating.

Whatever you do, don't hurry into a decision. Take your time. There are plenty of properties for sale out there, so don't get caught in the 'scarcity' trap that vendors use to improve their profits.

Also try not to set yourself impossible schedules and deadlines to view and buy a property. A few days or a long weekend is rarely enough time to consider things properly or to do the necessary checks.

If you are retiring to Portugal, then you should still do some thorough research. If you are fit and able, living somewhere remote might not be a problem. However, if you have any medical issues then living somewhere closer to health centres and other amenities might be a wiser option.

Another factor to consider might be how you wish to spend your retirement. For some, a quiet life of gardening and reading in a countryside location is ideal. For others, a more active social life might be desirable. Check what is on offer to you in the areas you are looking at and whether this suits you.

It goes without saying that sound financial planning for your retirement is a must. The cost of living in Portugal, especially in certain areas, is no longer as cheap as it used to be and one should always take inflation into account. The fluctuation in the value of Sterling to the

Euro has also meant that many retirees have struggled over the last few years to make ends meet, and some have even had to sell up and return home.

Speak to an expert financial consultant, who is knowledgeable about both Portugal and your country of origin, in terms of making the most out of your pension or other savings and investments. You should also consider discussing your tax liabilities, and estate planning and inheritance.

Learning Portuguese

Learning Portuguese is crucial, unless you want to live in an 'expat bubble' and not integrate, or have no wish to understand anything about the society in which you are living.

To rely on other people to do things for you is also very annoying and frustrating, and in the unfortunate event of an emergency occurring, it could be dangerous or even life threatening if you can't speak Portuguese. Learning the language can also help prevent you from being taken advantage of.

You should not only consider the benefits to you, but the fact that many Portuguese natives will find it extremely impolite and somewhat arrogant, if you are making no effort to speak to them in their language.

While tourist areas and more cosmopolitan towns and cities may have many English speakers to hand, small towns and villages will not. Government offices and authorities will rarely deal with you in English, and if you attempt to write communications in English you may well get a terse reply telling you that the working language of Portugal is Portuguese!

I have heard many an expat excuse, for example: the Portuguese like to practise their English, the world language is now English, they always reply back to me in English when I try to speak Portuguese, it is a difficult language, we don't have time as we've been so busy since arriving. The list is endless.

It is no good waiting until you are living in Portugal to learn and hoping you will just pick it up. You won't! You should start learning many months before your permanent arrival and keep doing it after your relocation. You cannot avoid studying if you really want to learn a new skill.

If you are not going to learn the language, or really feel you can't (although quite often people convince themselves they can't do things when it isn't actually the case) then you must seriously consider whether you should be moving in the first place.

OK, I have been hard on you – so what are my tips for making it easier to learn Portuguese?

- There are many language books, CDs and online courses out there. Some are better than others and some may suit people better than others.

Buying a few different courses and alternating them, while expensive, may help to keep things fresh and widen your vocabulary and grammar.

- The key is little and often. Studying 15 to 20 minutes a day is far better than an hour or two once or twice a week. You will retain a lot more and not find yourself getting bogged down with it and bored. You are also more likely to make that amount of time available each day and not find excuses for doing something else.

- If possible, try to find a private, native-speaking teacher and either attend a class, or preferably one-to-one lessons, so that you can study at your own pace.

- Study with a spouse, partner or friend for motivational purposes. If you both know there is a time set and that someone else is relying on you, you will be less likely to skip it and do something else.

- Try to find a non-English-speaking friend or friends.

- Watch Portuguese TV and listen to Portuguese radio. However awful some of the programmes might be, you will be amazed at how much sinks in after a while. Portuguese *telenovelas* (soap operas) are excellent for this. The language used is generally of the everyday type and you can usually follow the simple plots and story lines with ease. Most films are subtitled in Portugal and not dubbed, so this makes it even better. You can listen to English and read Portuguese.

- Don't worry about making mistakes and being perfect. *Just do it!* You won't learn if you don't make mistakes. Think of how many mistakes you hear when foreigners are trying to learn to speak English. Do you make fun of them? No. In general most people are appreciative of others making the effort to learn their language. Plus, it can be real fun.

- If someone replies to you in English, just keep speaking Portuguese, or if need be, ask them politely if they would mind not speaking to you in English.

- If you have certain jobs or shopping to do the next day, or later the same day, do a bit of homework before you go out. Make a list of the verbs and vocabulary you might need and learn them and take the list with you for support. Many situations are quite similar, so once you've learnt a few stock phrases you can use them again and again.

- If you forget a word, then remember that you may be able to use a few other words to describe the one you've forgotten and most of the time

you will get offered the word, or at least the
person you are speaking to will understand you.

CASE STUDY: LUCY PEPPER

When I was 20, I came to Portugal on a field trip as an art student. We spent two weeks in Porto and painted and drew in the city and in some of the vineyards along the length of the Douro. Porto was stinky and decaying, and the Douro unspeakably beautiful. We were fed proper Portuguese food: boiled *bacalhau* (codfish), with olives and chickpeas, and a chicken foot stew that offended the vegetarians' tender hearts. We travelled on a train with open doors; if you were mad enough you could dangle your feet out while you sat on the entrance step. We danced in the grapes with farmhands, whose deluded foreman earlier in the day had been supplying me with tots of *aguardente*, *moscatel* and port while I painted the hillsides. This was a British art student he was trying to get drunk...

I fell in love with Portugal. I have a sketchbook from that trip with the note "I will live in Portugal one day".

Eight years later, and having totally forgotten that note, I met my Portuguese boyfriend. A couple of years after that, I left London for Portugal with our 10-week-old daughter and a head full of ideas of what Portugal was and what life there would be.

We lived in the village where my boyfriend's family had lived for the past 20 years. Azeitão was about 35 kilometres from Lisbon and 15 from Setúbal, and I assumed it would be the archetypal Portuguese village of the collective British dream. What it is, however, is a sprawling suburb made up of five or six hamlets that have crept together over time and grown exponentially since the 1970s. The central village, Vila Nogueira de Azeitão, is still a jewel, albeit a bit of a crusty jewel with the edges knocked off, but much of the rest of the area is characterless 'burb populated by those drawn by the fashionable fame the area has mysteriously gained. If you squint, you can still see the splendour of the place.

After 10 years, we moved into a hamlet four kilometres away, inside the Parque Natural, which *is* the Portuguese village of our dreams. We've been here a while now and are just about to fix the place up and steeling ourselves for all the dealings with the council.

I arrived in 1999 with 'Learn Portuguese in Three Months'-level Portuguese. I soon realised that I'd need 'Talk Like a Native'-level Portuguese if I was to defend myself from the mother-in-law. My *sogra* is a hard-working woman with her heart in the right place, but she does like to *help*. Like many Portuguese of a certain generation, whose first exposure to the English consisted of the vacuous rich in Cascais and Estoril of the 1950s, she didn't think an Englishwoman would be capable of much beyond waking mid-morning and ringing the bell for the servant to bring her breakfast. Luckily, I have an ear for languages and it didn't take long to be able to speak Portuguese pretty well. That was the best thing I ever did. Learning the language properly opened up this country for me. I speak

Portuguese fluently, and live a totally integrated life in Portugal, spending 50 percent of my time talking, writing and thinking in Portuguese. My kids go to Portuguese schools. I work in Portuguese. The majority of my friends are Portuguese. In fact, it took me five years to meet any other foreigners nearby.

The culture shock and madness of a new country, and no one to share this with, led me to start a blog in 2003, an anonymous one, where I wrote and railed against the insanities of this place. I drew the pictures too. They didn't like that. My fictitious and exaggerated persona quickly became infamous in the Portuguese blogosphere, and known to many as 'that dreadful English woman'. I received many horrified emails of "How *dare* you?" but many more "Oh, God, you're *so* right" from Portuguese readers... And that's how I got back into working again. I had thought the only way I'd ever be able to work as an illustrator again would be to write and illustrate some *Year in Provence* style book, 'quaintifying' a place for Londoners to dream about on cold nights, and hoping the fashion for such books hadn't waned and that I might get it published.

Working in Portugal is tough and the money is rubbish — and there's not much of it for an artist, even though the bar isn't that high. The bureaucracy also sucks, day-to-day life if you're raising kids and trying to work (i.e. living here, not holidaying) can be as stressful as it is in the UK, and life isn't much cheaper. But if you haven't a problem with any of the above, then Portugal *is* paradise on earth.

I have only one piece of coverall advice for anyone moving here: learn the language properly, and then keep learning it. Read newspapers and books, watch the TV (a bit, it is awful), and make friends beyond your estate agent. This is the only way you'll ever get to really *live* in Portugal and know that its culture is stuck in the past but grasping at the future, that its food can be glorious even if it looks disgusting, and that its people are as lovely, ghastly, intelligent, vain, generous, jealous and funny as the people of anywhere else in the world. If only you'd learn the language, you'd know that.

Lucy Pepper, Azeitão
www.lucypepper.com

The Buying Process At-a-Glance

1. At Home — Planning and Research
2. In Portugal — Research Trip
3. At Home — Organise Buying Trip
4. In Portugal — Buying Trip
5. Finalise Purchase

Decide Why You're Buying

☐ Investment. ☐ For family.
☐ Rental. ☐ To live.
☐ Holidays.

Determine Finance

☐ Mortgage/remortgage. ☐ Sell something/cash in
☐ Staged financing. stocks or options.
☐ Credit cards. ☐ Get financial advice.

Do Research

☐ Read this book.
☐ Check property listings.
☐ Check credentials of estate agents, solicitors,
builders/developers, architects, etc.
☐ Research locations.

Make Criteria

Where? ☐Town/city ☐Countryside ☐Coast ☐Village
Transport? ☐Driving ☐Trains ☐Airports ☐Motorways
Amenities? ☐Hospitals ☐Schools ☐Shops ☐Nightlife
Type? ☐Self-build ☐New build ☐Off-plan ☐Resale

Make Specification

Size? ☐Bedrooms ☐Bathrooms ☐Garage
Outdoor space? ☐Garden ☐Patio/terrace ☐Pool

Arrange Research Trip

☐ Flights.
☐ Accommodation.
☐ Travel/car hire.
☐ Meetings – agent, vendor, solicitor, builder, etc.

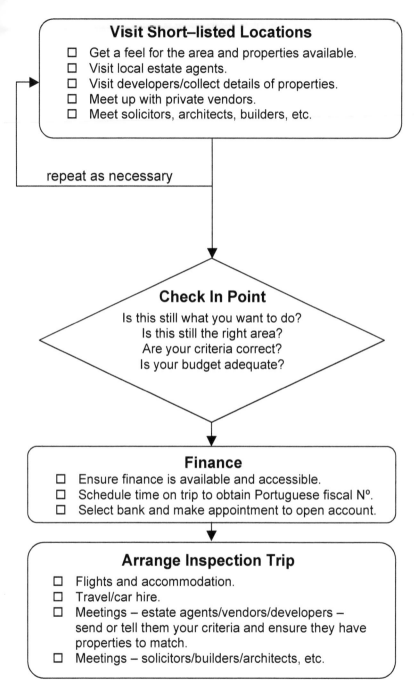

Visit Short–listed Locations

☐ Get a feel for the area and properties available.
☐ Visit local estate agents.
☐ Visit developers/collect details of properties.
☐ Meet up with private vendors.
☐ Meet solicitors, architects, builders, etc.

repeat as necessary

Check In Point

Is this still what you want to do?
Is this still the right area?
Are your criteria correct?
Is your budget adequate?

Finance

☐ Ensure finance is available and accessible.
☐ Schedule time on trip to obtain Portuguese fiscal Nº.
☐ Select bank and make appointment to open account.

Arrange Inspection Trip

☐ Flights and accommodation.
☐ Travel/car hire.
☐ Meetings – estate agents/vendors/developers –
   send or tell them your criteria and ensure they have
   properties to match.
☐ Meetings – solicitors/builders/architects, etc.

Viewings With Estate Agents/Vendors/Developers

☐ Be clear on criteria.
☐ Take trusted translator (if you need one).
☐ Take camera and video camera – take lots of photos and video footage to help you decide later.
☐ Make notes & use property check list in appendix.

Make Short List

☐ Compare each property against original criteria.
☐ Reject any obvious properties.
☐ Revisit the properties alone – at different times.
☐ Say 'Hi' to the neighbours and find out local gossip.
☐ Check out local amenities.
☐ Do your own checks – is the paperwork correct? Who owns it? Can you do renovations? Is the property structurally sound? Etc.

Check In Point

Does the vendor own the house?
Does the agent have a valid AMI Nº?
Does the developer have a valid Alvará Nº?
Does the solicitor have a valid Cédula Nº?

Buy Property

☐ Searches, surveys and promissory contract drawn up.
☐ Engage solicitor/translator/surveyor/builder.
☐ Sign promissory contract and pay deposit.
☐ Get certified copies of documents and IDs to present to notary and proof that IMT has been paid.
☐ Sign final deed and pay balance (12-18 weeks approx).
☐ Property registered at land registry.
☐ Receive certified copies of all documents and change of utility contracts.

Off-Plan, New Build, Resale or Self-Build

People have many different requirements and tastes when it comes to buying property and certain approaches may suit you better than others. In order to help you choose the right approach, I've provided a list of the pros and cons for each type of build. There may be some overlap between off-plan and new build, depending at what stage you are buying these types of properties. Also, a resale property that is virtually a ruin will have much the same pros and cons as a self-build.

Off-Plan

Pros:
- ✓ You will be moving into a brand new property with brand new fittings.
- ✓ You can usually choose your own bathroom suites, kitchen, tiles, paint, heating systems and other fittings.
- ✓ You may be able to alter some things at the design stage, such as an interior room layout, subject to planning permission via the architect.
- ✓ If one of several properties on a complex, you will get a better choice if you buy early on, e.g. size, shape, design, views, etc.

✓ In most cases, you are buying at a discount, that is, the price of the property you are buying at now will be less than it would be if already built. This is usually due to the developer wanting to attract investors to help finance the construction. Some people even sell the property on before completion to make a profit.

✓ Stage payments allow you to spread the cost of your purchase.

✓ You will get a five-year warranty against structural defects on completion.

Cons:

✗ The builder could go bust and you will be left with an unfinished property.

✗ The builder could go bust after your property is finished and, therefore, it could be left on an unfinished development/urbanisation.

✗ The communal areas are often the last to be finished and, therefore, it could be hard to rent out the property for quite some time, should you wish to do so.

✗ If the project is in its early stages or it overruns (which projects invariably do) then you could be waiting for quite some time before moving in and/or renting it out.

✗ Building work could still be continuing around you for some time after you move in and the dust, dirt and noise that goes with it. Once again this could affect its rental potential early on.

✘   If you buy in the early stages or before construction has even started, then you may not have a true idea of what it will really end up looking like.

New Build

Pros:

✓   The property is completely finished and you can move in straight away.

✓   If on an existing development, the infrastructure and facilities are likely to be in place.

✓   The building work in the area is usually finished and, therefore, it is quieter, cleaner and easier to rent the property.

✓   You will have a five-year warranty against structural defects.

✓   It is less likely that the property will have any of the maintenance issues that you might have with an older property.

✓   The fittings will be new.

Cons:

✘   Newer properties tend to have less land and are more likely to be on a development or urbanisation, which you may not like.

✘   The property is less likely to have the charm or character of an older one.

✗ You will have had no input on the choice of fittings unless you have agreed to buy it before it has been fully completed.

Resale

Pros:

✓ The property is completely finished and you can move in straight away. Therefore, less waiting time.

✓ You can negotiate on the price a lot more.

✓ If on a development, the infrastructure and facilities are likely to be well established.

✓ If the property has gardens, they are also likely to be well established.

✓ You can see exactly what you are getting and most problems will have been resolved.

✓ Older properties are more likely to have character and charm and also more land.

✓ More varied choice and availability.

Cons:

✗ There will be no builder's warranty, if older than five years.

✗ There might be more maintenance issues and renovation works to do, especially on older properties.

✗ More variability in prices with some owners holding out for well over the market value for their properties.

Self-Build

Pros:

✓ You can choose the plot where you wish to have your home built.

✓ While, of course, having to abide by the local planning regulations, you will have complete freedom to design your house.

✓ You can select the architect and builder of your choice and choose all the materials and fittings.

✓ You can be a lot more involved in the building process from start to finish.

✓ Stage payments allow you to spread the cost of your purchase.

✓ Everything will be brand new and tailor-made.

✓ You will get a five-year warranty against structural defects on completion.

Cons:

✗ 'Red tape' and general overbearing bureaucracy in Portugal, which at times might leave you exasperated and frustrated.

✗ A long waiting time for each stage to be completed and until you can finally move in.

✗ Choosing an unreliable architect and/or builder, or those whose working methods you turn out not to like.

✗   If you are not in the country, you will need to employ a project manager to keep an eye on progress.

✗   The builder could go bust and you will be left with an unfinished property.

✗   Costs can easily escalate and deadlines can slip without careful and consistent project management.

Location

One of the biggest regrets people, especially permanent residents, have in relation to buying property in Portugal is that they chose the wrong location.

Choosing the right location for your needs is essential and must be very carefully considered.

As previously discussed in the *Relocating* chapter, those wishing to buy a property as a holiday home, or those wishing to buy to let, will often have completely different needs from those looking to permanently relocate.

Those of retirement age may also have different requirements in comparison to younger couples with children, who may need to work.

In order to help you decide, I have provided a list of the pros and cons for each type of location. However, please bear in mind that this is a general list and that in Portugal there is often little difference between what constitutes a small town and a large village.

As with anything in life, it is always best to experience things for yourself.

Countryside

Pros:

✓   Peace and tranquillity.

✓   No hustle and bustle.

✓   Freedom and privacy to do as you wish.

✓   Self-sufficiency is possible.

✓   Closer to nature and nice scenery.

✓   Cheaper to buy than in coastal or city locations.

✓   Often lots of land and larger sized properties.

✓   Less crime.

Cons:

✗   Car is essential to go anywhere and a back-up car might also be required in case one breaks down.

✗   Often further away from the nearest shops, bars, restaurants, amenities and medical services.

✗   Poor (if any) public transport.

✗   Bad roads: narrow, sometimes hilly with poor surfaces.

✗   Poor or no utility services.

✗   Climate extremes: hotter in the summer and colder in the winter, often with strong winds, if on a hilltop.

✗   Fires more likely.

✗   Solitude, remoteness and loneliness.

✗   Harder to rent out and sell than coastal/city property.

✗   Unlikely to find work locally.

✗   Harder to maintain land and property, as well as more costly.

Villages

Pros:

✓   Neighbours around to help if you have a problem.

✓   Community spirit once you've been accepted into the village.

✓   More likely to experience the 'real' Portugal.

✓   Small shops, bars, restaurants, minor services and amenities.

✓   Public transport to the nearest town (although may be quite sporadic).

✓   Cheaper to buy than in coastal or city locations.

✓   Less crime.

Cons:

✗   Villagers less likely to speak English, so you will need to learn Portuguese in order to fully integrate.

✗   Often takes a long time to be fully accepted into the community and people tend to want to know your business.

✗   Poor utility services.

✗   Harder to rent out than coastal/city property.

✗ Less likely to find work locally.

✗ If you have children, they may have to travel to the nearest town for school, and for the elderly and infirm it may be too far from medical services.

Coast

Pros:

✓ Sea breeze helps make the summer heat more bearable.

✓ Usually reliable public transport.

✓ Good utility services.

✓ Close to shops, bars, restaurants, amenities and medical services.

✓ Entertainment and nightlife, especially in the summer.

✓ More likely to find English speakers.

✓ Easier to sell.

✓ Easier to rent out, especially in the summer.

✓ Easier to find work.

Cons:

✗ Can be a ghost town in the winter when many businesses close for their annual break.

✗ Parking problems and traffic congestion in the summer.

✗ Noise from holidaymakers, bars, restaurants and traffic in the summer.

✘ Overcrowded beaches, and packed restaurants and bars in the summer.

✘ Property is more expensive to buy.

✘ More crime.

Towns & Cities

Pros:

✓ Close to all kinds of businesses, shops, bars, restaurants, amenities and medical services.

✓ Entertainment, culture and nightlife.

✓ More likely to find English speakers.

✓ Good public transport.

✓ Good utility services.

✓ Easier to rent out, especially long-term.

✓ Easier to find work.

Cons:

✘ Noise from neighbours, pedestrians and traffic.

✘ Parking problems and traffic congestion.

✘ No community spirit.

✘ Lack of green spaces.

✘ Expensive to buy.

✘ Small plot sizes and properties.

✘ More crime.

✘ More hustle and bustle, and possibly stress.

CASE STUDY: EMMA CRABTREE

I'm Emma Crabtree and I live in Condeixa-a-Velha, Central Portugal, with my husband Lawrence. We have been in Portugal since 2004.

We originally relocated from our one-bedroom townhouse in South London to a large, detached house in a small and typical Portuguese village in the Beira Litoral, where we were the only English-speaking couple. We'd both made lists of towns we'd like to live in or close to and Coimbra, which is our district capital, was the only place that had made it onto both our lists! We knew that Portugal was where we wanted to live many, many years ago. I would say that the planning and preparation we did before leaving London has been the key to our success. We knew the country, the systems and the bureaucracy well before making the final commitment of buying a property. My first tip would be *plan ahead* — do your research and make contingency plans.

The house we bought was advertised through local agents and we viewed it, and many others, while we were in Portugal for two weeks during Euro 2004. Although we had researched and viewed other properties through expat agents, this company had properties that met our budget and ticked more boxes than any other agent. We bought through our lawyer, acting with power of attorney, and moved in September. Although the house came only partly furnished, we didn't take our furniture from the UK.

This was a mistake as there isn't the choice available in Portugal as there is in the UK. Furniture and white goods can be very expensive and there are very few second-hand stores along the high street. No Oxfam, Help the Aged or RSPCA stores here!

Our honeymoon period didn't last long. The summer extended into mid-October, and then it rained and rained. There's a reason Portugal is so green and has such a wonderful diversity of flora and fauna! And the winter was bitterly cold. Our house did not have central heating and we only installed a fireplace in late November, by which time friends had been to visit and froze most of the time. This cycle of glorious summers followed by wet and very cold winters has continued throughout our time in Portugal. So my second tip would be to ensure you have some sort of central heating in your home, wherever you end up. You won't use it from April to October, but you *will* need it at some stage!

The neighbours couldn't have been more generous, welcoming and kind and we have made friends who will be with us for life. I had read that the Portuguese are embarrassed about their way of living and won't take you into their homes. Not our villagers! We lunched and dined with our new neighbours within six weeks of moving in and were forever having people over for coffee. In hindsight, however, the village wasn't right for us. You can take the girl out of the city (15 years working and breathing London life), but can you take the city out of the girl? Our village had no facilities and the nearest supermarket was a 20-minute drive away. I was isolated and felt lonely. My third tip, therefore, is to know oneself. Are you absolutely sure that being in a remote, albeit gorgeous, stone cottage, alone, with snowed-in roads is for you?

It was at this time that I started my business, Red Box Virtual Office. Initially this was to give me something to do and to provide us with an income. Neither of us are near to retirement age and gardening can only take up so much of your time, especially over the winter. I'm what is known as a virtual assistant and my clients have been based in the US, Middle East, UK, Europe and Australia. The majority of my tasks are administration based: client care, customer service, sourcing and procurement, email management and so on. The tasks may vary, but what I fundamentally do never changes: I provide individuals and small businesses with support when they need it most. From starting off providing spreadsheets for my mum, I now run a small, but perfectly functional company for entrepreneurs and small businesses who are based somewhere other than in Condeixa-a-Velha.

There were several reasons for moving from our village. Not least of which was that I couldn't rely on the telephone or electricity service and these are very important utilities to have when running an online business. We were fortunate to advertise and sell our house within four months.

Since that time, we have bought two further properties, one of which we renovated and where we are living now; the other we sold. Our new house is well located for Red Box; Coimbra is just a 10-minute drive away and the A1 connects me with Porto and Lisbon within an hour or so. I achieve so much more now — including networking, lunches and dinners — and have begun to attract Portuguese businesses too. I would recommend thinking about what you can do to earn a living, or at least fill your days, if you are relocating and under the age of 70. What transferable skills do you have? What work experience? Lawrence is now a trained TEFL teacher, but his background is in social housing. Unemployment is high here, even among the well trained and qualified, and the cost of living is not as cheap as it used to be. Your nest egg will be nibbled away by all those *pastel de nata* (custard tart) stops you make each week.

One of the reasons new immigrants find themselves in difficulty is because they have bought a property without being able to speak the language and without independent advice. I'd highly recommend taking language classes (my fourth tip) both before relocating and once you are settled in Portugal. We took classes before, during and after our move, culminating at the University of Coimbra. It is frequently remarked by my Portuguese friends that the English, or indeed other nationalities, don't speak Portuguese and it annoys and frustrates them. Couple this with the fact that the majority of council employees you will have to deal with in small towns won't speak English, and you will see why being able to understand and be understood is crucial.

Portugal is a country of contradictions and I liken it to the UK in the 1960s. It is an incredibly beautiful country, but littering and roadside dumping are rife. The Portuguese adore children, but their attitude towards animals (abandoning them or not having them neutered) is backward. There's live bull fighting on the TV and villagers will butcher their own livestock. Portuguese women will smoke and drink through their pregnancies and take their babies into smoky bars, and there are jobsworths wherever you go. These are all issues that you need to take on board before moving to Portugal.

Third property lucky: we are happy in our small, bijou house with its enormous garden and great neighbours. We can walk to bars and restaurants and have all the amenities you may need on our doorstep. The Portuguese way of life, though it can be incredibly frustrating, suits us. It's not a stress-free life — anyone who has to deal with the local finance office will tell you that — but we are incredibly fortunate to have found somewhere we both feel comfortable and welcomed.

Emma Crabtree, Condeixa-a-Velha
www.redboxvirtualoffice.com

Regions of Portugal

For the purpose of this property-buying guide I have divided Portugal into five main regions:

- North
- Centre
- Lisbon
- Alentejo
- Algarve

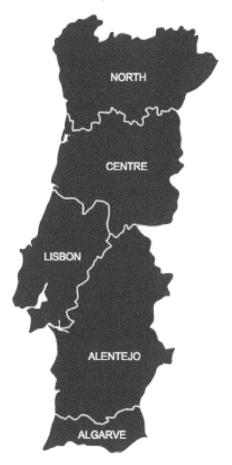

North

Not everyone who is thinking of relocating abroad is looking for endless hours of heat and sunshine. In fact, many people don't enjoy the extreme summer temperatures that can be found in some parts of Southern Europe. If you simply want a different and much more affordable and laidback lifestyle, then Northern Portugal might just be the answer.

The North consists of the Costa Verde (Green Coast), which is situated in the north-west and includes the provinces of Minho and the Douro coast, and part of the Montanhas (Mountains) in the north-east known as Trás-os-Montes.

The Minho borders the Galician province of Spain and it is often said that it bears more of a resemblance to its Spanish neighbour than Portugal. They both share some Celtic customs and there is a slight blurring of accents, for example the Portuguese in this area pronounce the letter 'v' as a 'b' as in Spain.

It is the greenest part of Portugal, mainly due to the large amount of rainfall in the region. The countryside is lush with rolling hills and mountains, woods and pine forests, fertile valleys and vineyards, and there are many unspoilt, long, sandy beaches and quiet coves. The landscape is like a patchwork quilt of small farms and houses, and there are some very beautiful stately homes and mansions, as well as ancient castles dotted about.

The Minho hasn't changed much in hundreds of years and is still a very conservative, rural and traditional region. In fact, you can still see oxen pulling carts to plough fields. Similarly, Trás-os-Montes, the most backward and poorest province in Portugal, seems to be lost in a medieval time warp with people washing their clothes in streams and some homes without mains electricity.

Four main rivers can be found in the region: the Rio Lima, the Rio Minho (which forms the border with Spain), the Rio Tâmega and the Rio Douro.

A wine known as *vinho verde* (green wine) is produced in the Minho, and in Porto, Portugal's second largest city, the famous *vinho do Porto* (Port wine) is made.

The main cities and towns in this region are Braga, Bragança, Chaves, Guimarães, Porto, Viana do Castelo and Vila Real.

The region is home to some of the most impressive historic centres in Portugal. Guimarães is the birthplace of the country and the beautiful Ponte de Lima is a regular host to the finance ministers of Europe. The spectacular national parks (Peneda Gerês in particular) contain many areas of protected wildlife and there are even wolves still residing in the mountains.

The famous, Portuguese cockerel symbol was born in Barcelos in this region and dates back to a 14th-century legend.

Portugal's longest motorway, the A1, which goes from Lisbon to Porto, enters this region and then connects with the A3 towards Braga. There is also a coastal road, which goes through Vila do Conde until Valença.

As well as the improved road networks in the region, there are good railway links to Porto, and Vigo across the border in Spain, and with regular flights to Porto from the UK and the airport at Vigo less than an hour's drive away, access to the region from other parts of Europe has never been better. This is with the exception of Trás-os-Montes, which has a rather poor road network and a limited public transport system.

Northern Portugal has seen little in the way of tourism, but visitors are increasing year on year. Viana do Castelo, the largest and main town in Minho province, is known as the folklore capital and is an attraction to outsiders for its many festivals, especially in the summer months. Much of the coastal area between Porto and Caminha is also now showing signs of holiday developments.

Many surfers prefer the challenges of the Atlantic Ocean further north and there are a large number of other water sports enjoyed, for example canoeing and boating. Climbing, hiking and fishing are also popular throughout the whole region.

The climate in the Costa Verde area is very damp and more akin to Northern Europe and certainly less reliable than more southerly parts of Portugal. However, the summers can still be very warm and pleasant, and many people prefer the beauty of the unspoilt countryside and fresh air to the more brown, arid and occasionally oppressive south.

Being mountainous, Trás-os-Montes is naturally more extreme in climatic conditions and can have particularly long, cold winters. Locals have been known to refer to the weather as "nine months of winter and three months of hell!"

More and more foreign buyers are now coming to Northern Portugal for its quality of life and slower pace. There is also an interest in eco and self-sufficiency lifestyles. However, property prices, while cheaper than Lisbon and the Algarve, are quite expensive compared to the Central and Alentejo regions of Portugal. This is due to the fact that many Portuguese emigrants still retain houses in the region, as well as those that work in Lisbon who own weekend or holiday homes.

While the Minho is generally expensive, there are pockets that are cheaper as you move inland towards Monção, and up into the mountains. Some mountain villages, even as close as Arcos de Valdevez, can also be less expensive although perhaps still not quite as cheap as the central region. It would seem that the prices vary across the northern part of Portugal more than in other parts and naturally, those areas in which people want to live are more expensive than those which are more remote.

Porto has a fair number of foreigners, including British expatriates working in the Port wine industry and some teaching English as a foreign language. However, the large-scale emigration by Portuguese in this region perhaps gives some indication as to the likely employment opportunities.

Outside of Porto, the region is very poor and employment prospects bleak. As an expat, your chances of finding any sort of work are close to zero. Therefore, this is really a region for retirees or those with alternative income.

In general, there are more rural farmhouses and town property for sale, as opposed to new builds. Ruins or dilapidated old manor houses and tumbledown granite cottages are also available for renovation, especially in rural areas, as due to the large-scale emigration by local people over the years, a lot of properties have been left to fall into disrepair.

The region is ripe for investment and until the recent recession there was a fairly active property market, especially for renovation projects. Golfing and leisure resorts have also started to make their mark in the last few years, as well as some small-scale developments. However, due to strict planning restrictions in the region and many areas of protected status, it is unlikely that mass developments will emerge.

Areas worth looking at are Caminha, Esposende and Viana do Castelo on the Atlantic coast, as well as inland towards Ponte de Lima and Ponte da Barca, and in general along the Lima and Minho Valleys. In fact, Ponte da Barca experienced quite a mini boom, with many new flats being sold over the last few years to Portuguese returning from working in France in order to retire on their French pensions.

From Valença to Monção there are some interesting manor houses and around Terras de Bouro, the gateway to the Peneda Gerês National Park, and the entire southern part of this national park and its beautiful countryside are potential hotspots.

Guimarães is a little industrial, but a nice flat in the old town, or in Braga, which are trendy places to own a pied-à-terre could potentially be a good investment for renting out to staff or students at *the Universidade do Minho*.

While it would probably never make for a serious property investment, a little house inside the castle walls of Bragança might be an option for those really looking for somewhere different and fun. The properties are delightful, but the area is very remote and transport links are virtually non-existent.

Centre

The central region includes the provinces of Beira Alta, Beira Baixa and Beira Litoral. The Serra da Estrela, the highest mountains in Portugal, divide the Beira Alta and Beira Baixa.

This central area also includes what has become known as the Costa de Prata (Silver Coast). The name deriving from the fact that the sun's reflection on the sea gives a silvery light. It stretches from Porto down to Lisbon along the Atlantic coastline.

This region is probably the most diverse in Portugal with its rolling hills, wooded mountain areas, spectacular scenery, pine and eucalyptus trees, varied flora and fauna, and long, sandy beaches. It also has many unspoilt, little fishing towns and coastal villages and rural inland towns and villages. The region is also known for its many sites of historic, religious and architectural importance. It has two main rivers: the Rio Zêzere and Rio Mondego.

The main cities and towns in this region are: Aveiro, Caldas da Rainha, Castelo Branco, Coimbra, Leiria, Guarda, Óbidos, Tomar and Viseu. Other towns of note are Alcobaça, Batalha, Fátima, Figueira do Foz, Foz do Arelho, Nazaré, Peniche and São Martinho do Porto.

Coimbra is the university town of Portugal and has one of the oldest universities in continuous operation in Europe, founded in the 13th century.

Since the A8 motorway was completed, thereby reducing the drive from Lisbon's airport to under an hour, the region has really been opened up and in recent years has seen an explosion in foreign property buying, especially around the Óbidos area.

Porto's Francisco Sá Carneiro airport is also used by those residing in the more northern areas of this central region.

The A1 motorway passes close to Coimbra and the IP5 links Spain to Aveiro. In addition, the IC9 motorway, which links Tomar to the Costa de Prata, is now complete and has reduced the driving time between Tomar and Nazaré to around 50 minutes. Work is also finished on the IC3 extension (now known as the A13), a journey from Tomar to Coimbra taking 45 minutes.

While the region is well served by many major roads, you will find that the further from the beaten path you venture, the poorer the quality of the roads become. The road surfaces in some of the more remote and rural areas are often uneven, with lots of sharp bends and hills.

A reasonably good and inexpensive train service operates between many larger towns in Central Portugal and both Lisbon and the North. However, the high-speed rail link between Aveiro and Salamanca in Central Spain, which has been discussed for several years, seems to have been shelved for now, as have the other three proposed Spanish-Portuguese high-speed rail links.

As well as good transport links, the increasing popularity of Central Portugal has been due to its cheaper property prices in comparison to those of the more famous Algarve coastal region. In fact, according to the *Instituto Nacional de Estatística* it was the cheapest region in which to buy property in 2013. However, there can be quite a variation depending on what part of Central Portugal you wish to purchase in.

Moving inland, areas such as Tomar (a UNESCO world heritage site) and Abrantes situated near the beautiful Castelo do Bode (Portugal's second biggest reservoir) have become more and more popular for both holiday homes and permanent residence. The area has rolling hills, rivers and a plethora of quaint villages and towns to visit.

The Castelo do Bode lake, which spans 60 kilometres, not only contains an abundance of wild life, but is very popular for water sports, such as canoeing, fishing, scuba diving and water skiing, and there is demand from both the domestic market and from overseas buyers for properties close to the lake.

Despite the tightening of planning rules adjacent to water sources, such as rivers, lakes and reservoirs, making them more at a premium, it is still possible to purchase a reasonably priced home in the vicinity.

Many other social activities can be enjoyed in the Tomar and Abrantes areas and they also offer great facilities, services and amenities. Therefore, property prices tend to be slightly more expensive than areas found a little further north, such as in Penela, Lousã, Mirando do Corvo and Arganil.

These more northerly areas, while having stunning scenery and still being very popular, are more remote and do not have as many services and amenities. Therefore, you would have to weigh up the pros and cons, as well as your priorities.

Tomar now has a sizeable expat community and while not overly touristy you will perhaps find more English speakers than in the more remote areas in this region. This might help with your transition into Portugal if lack of proficiency in the language is a cause for concern and if you are thinking of any possible expat orientated business.

However, as with nearly all the regions in Portugal, employment is not at all easy to come by, so make sure you do your homework first if you need to make a living.

Due to the rise of interest in Central Portugal as a place to live, the government now offers free Portuguese classes for foreigners in some of the bigger towns, such as Caldas da Rainha, Tomar, Ferreira do Zêzere and Ansião.

In addition, there are several events created by expats that live in the region where you can be involved as much or as little as you wish, and many (retirees in particular) now help the local Portuguese with the preparations for their traditional festivals. Not only is this a good way to use up the extra free time that many retirees find themselves faced with but also a great way to become more integrated into the community.

Tourism in Central Portugal has developed rapidly, especially on the Costa de Prata, and it is now a strong alternative to the Algarve. This might also be an important consideration if you are hoping to get any rental income from your property.

While the climate is mild, it should be noted that the Atlantic waves tend to be fiercer (a surfer's paradise) and the water and air temperatures a few degrees cooler than in the Algarve.

The climate is quite variable in Central Portugal with the more northerly areas often being substantially colder during the winter, especially the nearer you get to the mountains. In fact, skiing and other winter sports are popular in the Serra da Estrela. Therefore, one has to consider the cost of heating against the price of a cheaper property in the long-term.

The cost of living can be cheaper in Central Portugal than, for example the Algarve and Lisbon. However, if you shop in the main supermarkets and chains, there will not be such a marked difference.

The region is very popular with expats wishing to adopt self-sufficiency, eco and alternative lifestyles and perhaps lends itself better to this than other parts of Portugal.

The property in this region is varied depending on your taste and budget and includes new builds on new developments, plots, seafront apartments, fishermen's cottages, resale properties in the towns, and farmhouses or ruins for renovation in the more inland, rural areas.

Central Portugal also has a number of golf courses and some property development in connection to this has already taken place, especially around Óbidos and the Costa de Prata area, for example: Bom Sucesso, a leisure resort, golf and spa; Quinta de Óbidos, a country club and equestrian centre with luxury lakeside villas; and Royal Óbidos, a spa and golf resort with both villas and apartments. Plans have also recently been approved for a golf course near the aqueduct in Tomar.

Lisbon

Lisbon includes not only the capital itself, but also the southern parts of Estremadura and Ribatejo provinces. It stretches from Torres Vedras in the north to Setúbal in the south.

Going west along the coast there are many stylish resorts, such as Estoril and Cascais with their top hotels, casino, big villas and nice beaches.

Inland to the northwest of these resorts and up into the hills, is Sintra (a UNESCO world heritage town) with its lush, green woodlands, breathtaking views, beautiful, gothic 'fairy tale' buildings and Moorish legacy.

To the south of the Rio Tejo (River Tagus), the region's main river, is Caparica and the Costa Azul (Blue Coast) with its largely unspoilt, long, sandy beaches and sheltered at the southern end of the peninsula by the Serra da Arrábida Mountains. Other towns of note in the region are Mafra and Sesimbra.

Lisbon is steeped in history and culture, and due to the fact that it is built on seven hills, it has amazing views wherever you go.

Lisbon is a small capital by European standards and is a city of total contrasts. From the quaint Alfama district (the oldest part of the city) with its narrow streets and rattling trams, the historic Moorish Castelo de São Jorge (St George's Castle) overlooking the city, and the many funiculars and elevators to the Expo area with its modern architecture and restaurants, the trendy Chiado and Bairro Alto districts with their cafés, bars and nightlife and the impressive Vasco da Gama and 25 de Abril (25th April) bridges spanning the Rio Tejo.

Despite its quaint, old-fashioned charms, some parts of Lisbon are very dilapidated and in dire need of renovation and repair. This is mainly due to the tight building restrictions, bureaucracy and archaic rental laws. However, efforts are now being made to change this and clean up the city's fading façades and structures.

The climate in this region tends to be a little cooler than the Algarve in the summer, largely due to the stronger westerly breezes off of the Atlantic. It also tends to be quite a bit colder and damper in the winter. However, by Northern European standards it is still fairly mild and is one of the warmest European capitals all year round.

The sea is never far away and with a variety of beaches to choose from — the long, sandy Caparica coast or the more rugged Guincho and Praia Grande, for instance — it is a popular destination for those who love water sports, especially surfing, windsurfing and kitesurfing.

Sintra has its own microclimate due to its hilly, but near coastal position and is often used as a getaway from the city down below during the long, hot summer months.

Lisbon has an excellent road network and public transport system, as one would expect with it being the capital city. Overground trains, trams, buses, ferries and a metro (underground) are all fairly cheap and reliable.

However, it does have very bad traffic and parking problems and it is only recently that the Lisbon authorities have considered building more car parks and insisted on underground parking being a requirement for all new buildings.

A proposal to create an infrastructure at Alcochete (south of Lisbon) to complement and take some of the strain off of Lisbon's rather old and outgrown Portela airport (known as the Portela+1 formula) was in the pipeline, with the idea being to transfer some of the low-cost flights to this modular airport, but this seems to have been shelved. Likewise, a high-speed rail link between Lisbon and Madrid in Spain has been dropped for the foreseeable future.

Most foreign buyers in this area tend to be those who are working in the capital, but there is also now a sizeable proportion buying second homes and relocating for other reasons, including retirement.

More multi-national companies are now in evidence in Lisbon, making employment prospects possible for many expats. However, it is still not an easy task to land a job and teaching English as a foreign language is really only one of the very few other options.

While property in Lisbon tends to be some of the most expensive in Portugal, it is still relatively cheap compared to many other European cities, and is, in fact, one of the more affordable capitals in Western Europe.

Popular areas are: Alcântara, Alfama, Bairro Alto, Belém, Bica, Campo de Ourique, Castelo, Chiado, Graça, Lapa, Principe Real, Rato and Santa Catarina.

The range of property is diverse. You can find traditional city apartments with character in Alfama,

Castelo and Graça, modern riverfront flats and penthouses at Parque de Nações in the Expo area, sleek apartments in Chiado, and family homes and even palaces in Lapa.

Other areas of choice for expats are along the 'Linha de Cascais' (also referred to as the Estoril Riviera) where you will find bigger houses with gardens, perhaps more suitable for family life in comparison to city centre apartments.

Sintra is another popular area and offers everything from country houses, castles, palaces, estates and villas to smaller village houses and apartments.

In order to find cheaper property and affordable renovation projects in this region, places north of Lisbon like Torres Vedras or south of the Rio Tejo near to Sesimbra and the Serra da Arrábida may offer what you are looking for.

However, it should be noted that in the southern half of the Setúbal Peninsula, which includes Azeitão, Palmela, Sesimbra, Quinta do Conde and Setúbal itself, the larger mansion houses with land are rather expensive and tend to stay in families for years, and there are far fewer of the types of ruins that you might find in Central Portugal and elsewhere.

The building regulations also tend to be very strict in this area with little scope for extending what is already there, and due to the *Parque Natural* the recent building boom south of Lisbon stops abruptly at this boundary.

Likewise, renovating older properties in Central Lisbon might prove to be somewhat difficult due to the very tight planning restrictions and an overbearing amount of red tape. While you can often change a property internally without too much of a problem, changing a façade will prove a totally different matter and in some cases, it will be impossible.

Long-term renting out of your property, if bought for investment purposes, is easier in Lisbon than many other parts of Portugal, and in recent months a huge holiday rental market inside Lisbon has started to emerge, as can be seen on sites like *www.airbnb.co.uk*.

There are also some prospects for holiday rentals along the Caparica coast, as well as the Costa Azul and Sintra. However, your market in these locations is much more likely to be native Portuguese, than foreign.

Outside of the 'Linha de Cascais' and Sintra there are relatively few expats, with just a scattering of British, German and Dutch and certainly no 'expat enclaves' or British cafés and shops.

One last, but major consideration if you are thinking of living south of the Rio Tejo, is that if you have to travel into Central Lisbon in the rush hour it will take you a very long time indeed. The bridges are notoriously jammed at peak hours and you will have to pay tolls to cross.

Alentejo

The Alentejo region is situated from the Rio Tejo (River Tagus) in the north until the Algarve in the south. It borders Spain in the East and the Atlantic in the West and includes the provinces of Alto Alentejo, Baixo Alentejo and most of Ribatejo.

The region covers nearly a third of Portugal and is the largest but least populated. It is also the region with the oldest population. It is characterised by its rolling hilly grasslands and wheat fields, wide-open spaces, vast agricultural estates, whitewashed villages, and walled towns with castles and hilltop forts.

The Alentejo also has many cork oak forests, numerous olive trees, fields of sunflowers, beautiful flora and fauna and is known for its horse and bull breeding. It has often been referred to as the 'bread basket' of Portugal.

Wine production is famous in this region with many wine *quintas* (farms) producing award-winning wines, such as *Esporão*.

Nature reserves and parks also exist with an abundance of birds, such as storks, herons, egrets and birds of prey, and the coastline is largely unspoilt with many beautiful, long, sandy beaches and wild, rugged cliffs and rocks.

Some of the main cities and towns in this region are: Beja, Elvas, Estremoz, Évora, Monsaraz, Moura, Portalegre, Serpa, Sines and Vila Viçosa.

Unless on the coast, where the Atlantic breezes help moderate the temperature, this is an extremely hot part of Portugal during the summer and is, in fact, one of the hottest places in Europe with temperatures often surpassing 40°C. Conversely, in the winter it is often very cold with temperatures close to freezing at night. The sea is also a little colder along the west coast in comparison to the Algarve.

The road network is reasonable in the Alentejo and the A2 motorway from Lisbon to the Algarve crosses the region, which makes travelling fairly quick and easy between all three. However, the new road (A26) that was being built between Beja and Sines was halted back in 2012 due to the fact that the forecasted traffic did not justify the cost of its creation and would provide no significant benefit to the economy.

Other than the *intercidade* (inter-city) train service between the Algarve and Lisbon, which stops at Funcheira, Grândola and Alcácer do Sal, the public transport system is generally poor.

A new airport was opened at Beja in April 2011, but at the time of writing plans were being considered to turn it back to cargo use only due to the lack of interest by any carriers to make regular flights there.

Until a few years ago, the Alentejo was somewhere that people mostly just drove through on the way to somewhere else, and the only second homebuyers were wealthy Portuguese from Lisbon, who purchased their *Alentejo Monte* (typically, a detached country property with agricultural land).

It was of little interest to foreign property buyers with the exception of more adventurous types and those looking for complete peace and solitude.

However, this has slowly changed and the Alentejo is now an area of interest for those wishing to be away from the busier Algarve coast and who are looking for substantially cheaper property and a more natural lifestyle.

Compared to the rest of Portugal (and certainly many other parts of Europe), prices in the Alentejo are relatively low with only the central region being cheaper.

However, as an expat, work in this part of Portugal is going to be very hard to find and unless you have some form of alternative income or are retired, you may well struggle. You will also generally find fewer English speakers here, in comparison to the Algarve or Lisbon.

Some have found a niche offering painting, horse riding, cycling and hiking/walking holidays, and if on the coast, then there may well be a market for renting, especially to Portuguese nationals from Lisbon and the North.

Tourism has gradually been increasing over the years with many Portuguese and overseas visitors now heading to the calmer, unspoilt Alentejo coastline in the summer rather than the livelier and bustling Algarve, and inland there has been a rise in rural tourism.

The more desolate coastline is also very popular with surfers and the region as a whole is attractive to those who like outdoor pursuits and nature. Other activities of interest include birdwatching, wine tasting and visiting the many sites of historical and cultural importance, for example Évora (a UNESCO world heritage site) and the ancient walled town of Marvão.

In August, the sleepy and rugged coastal resort of Zambujeira do Mar hosts one of the biggest music festivals in Portugal called the *Festa do Sudoeste* and the town becomes quite the party place. However, away from this period it reverts back to its quieter self and there is a three-kilometre long path from here until Porto de Pesca along which you can cycle or walk.

Zambujeira do Mar is also part of the *Parque Natural do Sudoeste Alentejano* (Natural Park of the Southwest Alentejo) and the *Costa Vicentina* (Vicentine Coast National Park). Other national parks in the region are the *Parque Natural da Serra de São Mamede* situated to the east of Portalegre and the *Parque Natural do Vale do Guadiana* near to Mértola in the South.

A little further along the coast, the small village of Vila Nova de Milfontes is another popular destination with its cobbled streets, beautiful beaches, waterfalls, hideaways, various water sports, paragliding and ecological tourism.

There are two major rivers in the region: the Rio Sado, which crosses the city of Alcácer do Sal and the Rio Guadiana, which also enters the Algarve where it forms a border with Spain. Along the Rio Sado you can see flamingos, dolphins and other wildlife. There is also one of the largest man-made reservoirs in Western Europe at Alqueva, which impounds the Rio Guadiana on the Évora-Beja border near Moura.

There is a large range of property in this region, from coastal apartments along the west coast, which stretches from the border with the Algarve to the Costa Azul (Blue Coast) south of Lisbon, to ruins for renovation, farmhouses, village properties, plots to build and brand new villas with pools. Properties in inland Alentejo are also likely to have a lot more land than in other parts of Portugal.

As far as golf developments are concerned, the Troia Resort in the Northern Alentejo (only an hour from Lisbon) still appears to be a popular location. However, it seems that several other projects that were in the pipeline have suffered due to the recession and financing issues, and at the time of writing they are still not completed.

Even if these and other projects continue in the future, it is unlikely that the Alentejo will become overdeveloped due to its many protected areas, especially along the coastline, and no doubt it will manage to retain its beauty and charm for those preferring a quieter and more remote existence.

Algarve

The Algarve is the most southern region of Portugal and is also a province in its own right.

The word Algarve comes from the Arabic, *Al Gharb* meaning 'The West' and everywhere you look you can still see the Moorish influences in the architecture, for this was the last region of Portugal to be reconquered.

Whitewashed houses with Moorish chimneys, traditional fishing villages, long, sandy beaches and coves and cliffs characterise this region, together with its hilly countryside dotted with almond, fig, olive, carob and citrus fruit trees. The Algarve also has a range of mountains called the Serra de Monchique, which border the Alentejo.

A lot of the Algarve has now become quite built up along the coastline with some overdevelopment certainly in evidence. In the summer some of the resorts are bustling and somewhat overcrowded.

However, if you travel to the far east and west of the region, as well as only a little way inland, you can still find more typical and unspoilt areas and those that disparage it as not being 'real' Portugal are somewhat misinformed.

Protected areas of natural beauty still exist in this region, with many nature reserves and a particularly wild and rugged western coastline. Surfing, walking, cycling, fishing, birdwatching, and of course, golf are activities especially enjoyed throughout the Algarve.

The climate in the Algarve is mild nearly all year round and boasts over 3000 hours of sunshine a year. During the peak summer months, temperatures can get very hot, especially inland, where it can be similar to the Alentejo. However, along the coast there is usually a cooling sea breeze, especially the further west you go.

Winters in the Algarve can be damp and chilly and to many people's surprise heating will definitely be required, as night-time temperatures can fall quite considerably with occasional frosts.

Sea temperatures, while warmer than other regions of Portugal, can still be quite cold, although travelling east towards Spain will see these temperatures rise a little, as the Mediterranean Sea exerts its influence on the Atlantic Ocean.

The main cities and towns in this region are: Albufeira, Faro, Lagos, Loulé, Olhão, Portimão, Silves, Tavira and Vilamoura.

The A2 motorway runs from Lisbon through the Alentejo right into the Algarve, where it joins up with the A22. This makes travelling between Lisbon and the Algarve fairly quick and easy. Other roads in the Algarve are generally good with the A22 motorway going all the way through from west to east and joining up with the Spanish motorway across the border.

Public transport is also adequate in the region and the *Alfa Pendular* and *intercidade* (inter-city) train services between Lisbon and the Algarve are very reliable, comfortable and inexpensive.

Faro airport is easily accessible from all parts of the Algarve, even the far west, and there are many daily budget flights operating from the UK, both charter and schedule.

The Algarve is the region which has always seen the most investment by foreign buyers and is still continuing to do so, largely due to its wonderful climate and laidback lifestyle.

However, due to the more expensive price of property, in comparison to other regions in Portugal, and the fact that for some, it has become a little too developed, it does now have a lot more competition on its hands.

It must be pointed out though that the overdevelopment is all relative and if you compare it with many other seaside destinations around the world, you will still find most of the Algarve to be largely unspoilt.

The recent recession and subsequent EU-IMF bailout affected the property market quite considerably in Portugal, and the Algarve suffered as much as anywhere in the country with a substantial fall in house prices. However, the region weathered the storm better than comparable regions in its neighbour, Spain, and on the positive side, this means that some properties out of reach to many just a few years back may now be more affordable and even some bargains had.

The reasons for people purchasing a property overseas are varied and therefore if the aim is to live permanently in the country for some time and not just for a quick return, then the Algarve will always be attractive to many and now could actually be a good time to start your property search.

The fact that it is a regular summer holiday favourite and top golfing destination will also help maintain it as a desirable area of Portugal and Europe in which to buy property, especially if one of the aims is to seek some rental income.

When the A22 motorway was extended a few years ago, the largely unspoilt west around Lagos, Luz and beyond, and the west coast saw a big surge in development albeit of low-density construction. However, the area still retains its charm and prices here will be cheaper than more central parts of the Algarve.

The Eastern Algarve, which has traditionally been a little cheaper than both central and western parts, likewise saw development near Tavira and Cabanas and also the Spanish border around Castro Marim, Monte Gordo and the River Guadiana. If regular trips into Spain appeal, this might be a factor with Seville less than an hour-and-a-half from the border.

The 'golden triangle' of Vilamoura, Vale do Lobo and Quinta do Lago, where you can find some of the most expensive property in Portugal, if not Europe, is still a big favourite for those with the money to buy there, and many celebrities and sports personalities own property in this area. The Formula One track at Portimão in Central Algarve also entices some.

If you don't have a need to be right near the coast and prefer to be away from the hubbub, especially in the summer months, then moving slightly inland to places like Silves (the old Moorish capital of the Algarve with its beautiful castle), Loulé, São Brás de Alportel and São Bartolomeu de Messines might be ideal. Here some fantastic properties can be found in scenic and peaceful countryside environments.

If you wish to be even further away and more mountainous terrains and retreats are your thing, then taking a trip up into Monchique and its surrounds to experience the wonderful views and fresher air could also be worth your while. Here the prices will be considerably cheaper.

If you need to work in Portugal or set up a business, then the Algarve is perhaps the easiest location in which to do so, as a large number of tourist and real estate jobs require English speakers. There is also a substantial English-speaking expat community. However, please re-read the *Relocating* chapter as even in the Algarve jobs are not so easy to come by now.

If getting to grips with the Portuguese language is a major issue for you, then this region of Portugal might also be favourable, as a majority of the Algarve population, especially the younger members, speak very good English, as well as often French and German.

You can find every type of property imaginable in the Algarve, from ruins with lots of land in the countryside to coastal apartments, and from new-build villas on large developments to plots and, of course, lots of resale property.

CASE STUDY: EMMA BRUNTON

Making an escape from the rat race had been my plan for five years before I left Sydney. I was a film producer, but I had strayed too far away from the film-making and documentaries that had drawn me to the industry in the first place. I was spending my days (and nights too, usually) in the deluded world of television commercials, saving otherwise useless products from obsolescence with a whole lot of window dressing and untruths. I was bored to death in meetings where the ad people ardently argued whether to serve the product sauce with rice or potatoes. Or by standing around at 3 A.M. watching a hamburger on a turntable under a jungle of lights while grown adults pondered if the bun looked soft enough. Was this important? Was it relevant to what was happening in the world? Was this my life?

So when I was fired for refusing to ask a colleague to cancel their holidays (nothing could be more important than finishing a half-made advert), I took it as a blessing. I knew my piggy bank wasn't full yet, but I also knew I might be stuck waiting another five years for the last 20 big ones to appear. It was time to jump in.

I did what had to be done. I sold my entire wardrobe on eBay. I would start my new life naked as a baby with low-cost-airline-approved cabin baggage.

First I went travelling in Asia, and then I visited friends around Europe. That done, I had a long list of countries to visit where I would look for something to do, like opening a café, or having a small hotel, or buying and renovating a house. I had researched some vague scenarios set in Croatia or Bulgaria, on a lake, with free-range chickens.

But first I had to visit Portugal. Years before I had left if off the itinerary of a round-the-Mediterranean trip, because, technically, it's not on the Mediterranean, and I still wanted to go there. I loved the place. I "oo-ed" and "ahh-ed" at the dilapidated architecture of the cities and stuffed my face with pastries. Somehow I could understand what people were saying and Portuguese flowed from my mouth like I had a Babel fish in my ear. I thought the Portuguese were the nicest people in the world. And oh bless! Look at the olive trees and the grape vines and the rows of stone walls... and all those adorable abandoned ruins with 'for sale' signs.

Yes Siree, I was sucked right in. I set myself up in a €15 a night hotel in Lisbon, and every day I'd cross Avenida da Liberdade to spend the day at an Internet café in the corner of an 18th-century ballroom. There I researched the property market and found houses I wanted to view. I researched building costs and the cost of living. And most importantly, I investigated what it would take for a non-EU national to get residency in Portugal.

Then I went out and looked at 34 houses. It went on for months. The trouble was, I had seen the house I wanted in the beginning, but the documents for the property were all wrong and the estate agent no help to me. So I kept looking, but never saw another house with the magic of that one. Eventually I came back to it and, with the help of another agent, got the ball rolling on the buying process and the rectification of the deeds.

Then I had to get out of Portugal in order to make my application for a visa. I went and lived in Berlin. Trying to buy a house and making an application for building works is made much harder by being out of the country. The visa process was arduous, with the embassy sending me away repeatedly to get more documentation and testing me to see if I would give up this dream of living in Portugal. It was a difficult time, but I don't regret living in Berlin for a minute because it is where I learned Portuguese.

As I don't speak German, group classes weren't an option. I eventually found an English-speaking Brazilian to be my *professora*. I struck gold. She had a real talent for teaching and enormous patience with me, and we became good friends. I had two hours of lessons a day and in six months we had completed an entire school curriculum of grammar. Not only did private lessons keep me focused and enthusiastic, but also my teacher helped me talk to the real estate agent, the architect and the embassy when problems got too much for me to handle.

After nine months I had a *projecto de arquitetura*, a *visto de residência* and finally the owner and I were ready to sign an *escritura*. I packed up again and moved back to Portugal. This time I went to live in the small town of Lousã in Central Portugal, not too far from my house. I had great fun driving around the mountains and the Aldeias do Xisto (my house has the same architectural style so characteristic of this region) and getting to know Central Portugal while living in a youth hostel, where I also made my first Portuguese friends.

After a few more legal hiccups (including the owner wanting to keep the keys for the property after I had paid for it), the house was finally mine. I spent a month cleaning, painting and killing fleas, and then I moved in.

The neighbours in my tiny, isolated village were overwhelmingly friendly and even persuaded me to adopt one of their puppies. I also had my cat from Australia shipped over, at great expense and hassle, but now we were a happy furry family. Despite everything we had been through, the old house still had the magic for me, and even today I look out of the window at the vista of olives trees and grapevines and sigh.

Hiding away in a remote village in Central Portugal did not stop the global financial crisis from visiting. It didn't happen overnight, but between the share markets plummeting and a huge swing in the Aussie dollar, I lost about half of my remaining money. It had been hard enough finding a builder who shared my vision, but now paying one to *build* my vision was almost impossible. So, much like every expat in Portugal, I put the brakes on spending and sat tight for a while. Instead of building I started writing, and while it didn't solve my financial dilemma, it did give my life a new, creative angle.

All of my vast Australian family and many Aussie friends came to see the house. Be warned, house-hunters: you can't keep the visitors away! Some were a bit shocked by my radical change of lifestyle, but many fell in love with the place. "It's so quiet!" "So unstressful!" "There's no TV!"

Then I met a fantastic English guy, fell in love and got married. We moved into his rented place for a year and started a serious bit of renovating on my old house. But instead of the project I had planned for, I could only do as much as my finances allowed. No matter how much planning there is with renovating old houses, it is very easy to misjudge how far your budget will go, as under every old stone is a surprise you weren't expecting.

Meanwhile, the economic situation in Portugal had continued to decline. There was no way to earn a proper living with so many businesses going under and such massive unemployment. We spent a lot of time trying to resurrect my husband's business and watched as many expats returned to their home countries. Eventually, I too decided it was necessary to go back to Australia to get work, while my husband stayed behind to continue his business and look after the house. And that's when disaster stuck.

On the first job I got back in Sydney I did my back in. After seven years digging holes and shifting stones, mixing mortar and pushing wheelbarrows, I broke my back standing still! I recovered enough to continue working in a different job, but it marked the beginning of the end of house building. After another six months in Portugal I needed more treatment, and we needed more money, so I came back to Sydney again, this time to find out that I definitely needed surgery. Now we are in the process of moving to Sydney for good.

I've heard of other people having their Portugal dreams ended for health reasons. It's not exactly something you can plan to avoid from the outset, but it is something you should be aware of when planning your relocation. Personally, I consistently found the Portuguese health service inadequate for my needs. Perhaps if you were in Porto or Lisbon and had a very good family doctor, you might be ok, but not even private health insurance will get you very far if you're in the countryside.

The most important piece of advice I can offer is not to underestimate how much money you really need for your adventure. Although the economic crises had a huge impact, I wish I had focussed on how to earn a living from the very start and had a disaster plan in place. After many years in Portugal I can see there are opportunities for business there, but there is also enormous risk with an economy that is so small and fragile.

The best option is not to cut all your ties with your motherland and to have a few sources of income to fall back on.

Emma Brunton, near Lousã

www.emmashouseinportugal.com

Real Estate Agents and Vendors

On deciding to buy a property in Portugal most people head straight for the local agents in the area that they are looking in or, if back in the UK, surf around the Internet to see what they can find. There is nothing wrong with either approach. However, do you really know who is doing the selling and whether they should be or not?

Whether you decide to buy a new build on a development, a resale property, a plot to build on or a countryside ruin, you should make sure of the reputation and credentials of those you are dealing with.

While there are those with a first-class reputation, and professionalism and integrity in their dealings, there are of course others, who unfortunately have no conscience or scruples, and who would sell you their grandmother if they could!

So, how can you really know? How can you find out about who you are dealing with?

While nothing is ever 100% certain in the property world, there are some checks you can make to safeguard yourself.

Checking Out Portuguese Agents

In Portugal, a real estate agent has to be registered and, therefore, have the appropriate insurance and professional qualifications. A registered agent is given a number. This is known as an *AMI N°* and is issued by *INCI (Instituto da Construção e do Imobiliário)*, who are the regulatory body for all estate agents in Portugal.

To check whether a real estate agent is registered and has an *AMI N°,* consult the *INCI* website at *www.inci.pt.*

Click on *Mediação Imobiliária* on the left-hand side, followed by *Consulta de Licenças de Mediação* also on the left-hand side and then on *Consulta de Licenças de Mediação Imobiliária* in the centre.

You can then insert all or any of the following: *AMI N° (N° Licença),* company fiscal N° *(NIPC)*, name *(Denominação)*, address *(Morada)*, postal code *(Código Postal)* or locality *(Localidade)* and click on search *(Pesquisar)* in the bottom right-hand corner. *Limpar* means to clear.

If you want to find all the registered real estate agents in a particular district *(Distrito)* or council area *(Concelho),* click on the arrows alongside the relevant boxes, highlight the area you want and then click on *Pesquisar.* By clicking on an individual agent you can check all their details, such as when their licence was issued *(Licença emitida em)*, their company fiscal N° *(NIPC)*, their insurance company *(Seguradora)* and the expiry date of their insurance *(Data de Validade do Seguro).*

It has been known for real estate agents to display a false *AMI Nº*. So, just because they *seem* to be legitimate, don't take it for granted — double check.

The *AMI Nº* should be displayed on their website (as well as the title *mediação imobiliária*) and on all company documentation. Agents should also carry an ID card issued by *INCI.*

Some real estate agents may also be members of *APEMIP.* This is an association for real estate agents in Portugal. The website can be viewed in both Portuguese and English at *www.apemip.pt.*

A real estate agent must be in possession of copies of all paperwork and documents relating to the property for sale. Information on these documents can be found in the *What's What* chapter.

Treat all real estate agents the same way. Just because they might be a fellow national and/or speak your language fluently, it doesn't make them any more reputable or trustworthy. Check them out.

More recently, if a real estate agent is involved in the sale of a property, then their name and details must also appear on the final deed *(escritura).* If you wish to check whether the real estate agent is a limited *(lda)* company and the details of that company, read the *Builders &*

Architects' chapter to find out how you can do this via the Internet on the *Portal da Empresa* website.

If you need to contact *INCI* to make further enquiries or to make a complaint, click on *Contactos* on the home page at the top under the banner.

Anyone offering a service to the public also needs a complaints book (*livro de reclamações*) and a real estate agent is no exception. You are entitled to request and complete this book (usually a pad in triplicate) at any time. Any entity being complained about has five working days in which to submit this complaint to the relevant competent authority.

Complaints can then be followed up online at *http://rtic.consumidor.pt* by clicking on *01 Consumidores e Operadores Económicos* and putting in your passport (or ID) number and complaint number (*Número da Reclamação),* which should be on your copy of the complaint form.

Remember, in Portugal, legal representatives are not permitted to act as real estate agents and sell properties.

Checking Out UK Agents

As well as Portuguese real estate agents, there are UK companies on the Internet that sell property and plots in Portugal. They are sometimes connected to a builder or developer and these, of course, will not be registered by *INCI.* Therefore, you should remember that you will not be protected by Portuguese Law should anything go wrong.

Some UK registered companies merely advertise properties and put you directly in touch with Portuguese registered agents or private owners.

Many of these companies are simply run from homes or behind other businesses and when you telephone or email them they will often put you in contact with someone in Portugal. Do your homework again. Check whether they are registered at Companies House in the UK.

Go to *www.companieshouse.gov.uk* and click on *Find company information* and then *Start now*. Enter the name of the company and click on *Search*.

A list will appear with companies of that name or similar. Click on the number of the company you are looking for and if they are registered correctly the company details, such as the registered office address, company number, date of incorporation, company type, nature of business, status, and accounting and return dates will be shown.

To find out more details, such as the directors' names and for copies of returns and accounts, you can click on 'Order information on this company' on the right-hand side, or telephone, write to or email Companies House. They charge a fee for this service.

Check also when you contact the real estate company in the UK, whether they have an office in Portugal and, therefore, the address, telephone numbers and email address for that office, as well as the name of the contact in Portugal.

There are also UK based companies with Portuguese real estate 'arms' doing viewing trips for a very cheap fee per person. However, a long weekend is rarely enough time to view enough properties sufficiently. Secondly, they aren't giving you a good price on the viewing trip simply because they're nice. Their goal is to sell you property. So, if you do decide to go on one of these trips be prepared for their pressure selling tricks and don't let anyone rush you to make a decision.

Consider these companies in the same light as you would any other and make sure you do the necessary checks.

Checking Out Private Vendors

Of course there are people who prefer to sell privately. No problem in that. But check that the person selling the property actually owns it. It may sound bizarre, but there have been cases of people buying houses from individuals, who don't actually own them! Not very nice when the real owners come back to claim them.

Also, check how many people own the property. Quite often the title can be in the name of several family members and if one of them happens to be living overseas, it can be very difficult getting them all to agree to sell and sign. See the *Land Registry — Conservatória do Registo Predial* and *Notary — Cartório Notarial* sections of the *What's What* chapter to find out how you can check, regarding who the owners of a property are.

Other Checks You Should Carry Out

Check that the property you are buying is actually destined for habitation and not any other type of building. It should have a habitation licence or pre-1951 certificate, and, on the previous deeds, *caderneta* and land registry certificates, it should state *Casa de Habitação* and not any of the following as its main usage: garage (*garagem*), warehouse (*armazem*), storage building (*arrumos*), commercial use (*comercial*) or oil press (*lagar*). See the *What's What* chapter for more information on all these documents.

If you are buying a plot of land, in order to have a house built, then check that you can actually build on it. Even if there is already a ruin on the plot, don't just assume you can go ahead and build. Planning rules regularly change and land you cannot build on is of little value. Don't just take verbal confirmation from agents and others.

Check what type of land you are buying, that is, how it is classified. Is it urban and designated for construction? Or is it rustic, agricultural and/or ecological?

How is the land zoned? What size property can you build on it, or by how much can you extend what is already there?

Go to the local council *(câmara municipal)* to ask these questions and find out whether you will get approval for your intended project or works. Get anything they say confirmed in writing by asking for a viability of construction *(informação/comunicação prévia — viabilidade de construção).*

Check with your individual local council as to the period of validity of this document. It usually takes around a month to obtain and could last up to a year, but as things often change in Portugal make sure you confirm this and perhaps enlist the help of a local architect.

You can also ask to see the *PDM (Plano Diretor Municipal).* This is the municipal development plan and is renewed every 10 years. It states what can be built in different areas. Ask when it is due for renewal and if it is near its end, ask if they have a renewal one ready. Some local councils have this information online.

You can find your local council at www.cm-(your_town).pt, for example Faro council would be *www.cm-faro.pt.*

Remember that while, in a country like the UK, planning permission can take up to six weeks, in Portugal it could take anything up to a year! See the *Builders & Architects'* chapter for more on this.

In Portugal when the property for sale is either rustic *(prédio rústico)* or mixed, i.e. rustic and urban *(prédio misto*), the adjoining neighbours will have first refusal on it. This is called *Exercício de Direito de Preferência*. If you put in an offer for a property and the price and date for completion are agreed, then you should check that the neighbours have been notified and get it in writing from them that they have no interest in purchasing it.

The real estate agent should have done this for you, but double check. If not, they could have the right to claim the property at the agreed price several years down the line!

Check where the boundaries to the property are exactly situated. Get a map from the local council or from the *Direção-Geral do Território* (more on that in the *Maps* section of the *What's What* chapter) and walk the land with the owner, noting where the markers are. In the countryside the boundaries are usually denoted with large stone markers splashed with white paint.

The maps are not always as accurate as you might hope though, so if there are any doubts, ask for a surveyor to carry out a topographical survey and mark out the boundaries.

Check if there are any public rights of way that cross the property and if you wish to add a track or access road, that you will get permission from the local council to do so. If the track/road is going to cross anyone else's land, you will also need to seek their written permission. Make sure that you have complete and legal access to the property you wish to purchase.

Remember, a nice view can disappear instantly if somebody builds on it. If there is any land for sale in front of the property you are interested in purchasing, then you cannot guarantee that it will stay the way it is now forever.

Check that everything in the property works, for example: electricity, boilers, fitted appliances, heating and air-conditioning systems, and swimming pool equipment. Don't just take the vendor's and real estate agent's word for it. If the property has been built within the last five years, then ask to see the builder's guarantee. These are usually transferable to the new owner.

Also ask what will remain in the property as part of the sale. Some Portuguese owners will even take the kitchen sink with them, as well as all the light fittings and bulbs; so don't just make an assumption.

It is quite rare for foreign purchasers in Portugal to request property surveys if they are not requiring any form of bank loan and even then the banks tend to send an architect or engineer, as opposed to a trained surveyor. However, it is well worth considering getting a survey done, especially for older properties.

Remember to deal with buying a property in Portugal in exactly the same way as you would back home. Make sure if you are going to use a fellow national as the surveyor that they are knowledgeable in Portuguese construction methods and ask them if they have professional indemnity insurance. Ask them what will be included and what won't be included in the report.

Another option, which might be more cost effective, would be to ask a reputable builder to take a look at the property, as they will be able to give you an idea of the cost to repair or renovate any potential problems, something a surveyor may not be able to do.

Check what plans there are for the immediate area at the local council, in terms of developments, roads, shops, etc, which may be to your advantage, or conversely, have an adverse effect on the property. Also, check the *PDM* mentioned above to see what type of land you are surrounded by and the likely level of building to take place in the future.

If you wish to add a swimming pool to the property, or check about the legalities of an existing one, then see the *Swimming Pool Licences* section of the *What's What* chapter.

Recently, all properties within the water margins set out by the Portuguese government as public water domain need to be registered. A government department is in the process of drawing up a definitive map of the coasts and rivers, which will be published in 2016. You may need to check that this has been carried out if you have an interest in purchasing a property close to public water domain.

Other checks you should carry out can be found in the following chapters. A property purchase checklist can also be found at the back of the book.

NATIVE'S TIP

If you receive any objections or obstructions from the vendor or real estate agent in relation to any of the checks you wish to carry out then ask yourself what they may be hiding and whether you still want to go ahead with the purchase. There are plenty of properties out there. Think carefully!

CASE STUDY: MANDY DE AZEVEDO COUTINHO

In 2003, after 15 years of living and working in London for a number of renowned international real estate companies, luxury tour operators and villa rental companies covering Southern Europe, including Hamptons International, CV Travel and Abercrombie & Kent Villas, I moved to Lisbon.

My area of expertise was contracting holiday villas in France, Italy, Greece, Morocco, Spain and Portugal; but with a stronger connection to Portugal as I have dual Portuguese/British nationality.

The move came about after I found myself travelling more and more to Portugal. I discovered wonderfully charming tourist projects cropping up here and there and I began to fall in love with the country on a professional basis. At the same time, I was becoming increasingly tired of living in London.

Moving to Portugal wasn't that difficult for me, being that I am half Portuguese and bilingual. However, the exception to this was dealing with anything bureaucratic! Be warned, you can't just call the number of the required department and get the right advice as you might do in the UK. In Portugal, you need to make sure that you ask all the relevant questions (which you might not even know in the initial stages) or you will not be given all the necessary information. Reading and understanding the legal jargon, which is used excessively in Portugal, is also a test even for someone who did their schooling in Portuguese.

So my main advice would be don't try to do everything yourself on the cheap. Always get an expert on your side and get to know the ins and outs, making sure that the accountant or solicitor you choose is an expert in the area of your business. If you don't, you could find yourself caught up with all sorts of problems. For example, after my first year of business I had to pay a much higher tax bracket than I should have done, as my accountant was not aware of the running costs that could have been discounted from the total tax bill under my tax category.

Initially, I worked as an agent for Abercrombie & Kent Villas in Portugal, but after a few years I bit the bullet and decided to go it alone. Our trading platform and website (*amendoeirasemflor.com* - later renamed *almondblossom-rentalvillas.com*) offers a personalised booking service and a handpicked selection of holiday rentals in Portugal - all quite unique and recommended for very special reasons: location, charm, style or standard of service. However, most of my job is in fact taken up with advising property owners on how to go about setting up their villas for holiday rentals and what they should consider.

A lot of people buying a property in Portugal will be thinking about rental income and if it's worth it. Here is my list of top considerations to take on board:

i) Do consider what periods of the year you may want to use your holiday home bearing in mind that July and August are the months when you can charge the highest rental rates and most tour operators will also insist on some availability during this period to feature the property. On the plus side, May, June, September & October are lovely months to visit, as there are far less crowds and the weather is still mild.

ii) Don't expect to make a serious profit out of renting your holiday home. However, the rental income will potentially cover the running costs and pay for your own holidays there.

iii) Do work out the most competitive rental rates for your holiday home, taking into account similar properties in the same area. The cost of water, gas, electricity, bed linen and bathroom towel changes, supplying pool towels, basic maid service, garden and swimming pool maintenance, plus general everyday maintenance, should be included in the rental.

iv) Don't try to control the gross rental price your property is being rented out at via tour operators – they do the job of marketing the property and bringing clients to your front door and need to cover those costs. You should be happy with the net rental rate you have set for your holiday home and that it is paid on time.

v) Do include as many extra services as possible for added rental value, such as a cook service, a baby cot and high chair, pool heating, air-conditioning, etc. Even if not included in the initial rental fee, the availability on request of any of these services for an extra charge will generally add to the attraction of renting your property in comparison to others.

vi) Don't think you can get away with not obtaining a permit from the local council for renting your holiday home – tourism being one of Portugal's main industries has made the authorities pretty good at catching up with law breakers, and the fine for not having a rental licence versus the fee for having things legalised is just not worth it!

vii) Do take EU & Portuguese health & safety standards for renting holiday homes seriously – they are designed to protect both you and your clients. Some of these as are follows: full-length glass windows and doors or panels without frames must have warning stickers on them at both adult and child height; smoke detectors must be located throughout the property including all bedrooms, kitchen and communal living areas; there must be a fire extinguisher and fire blanket in the kitchen as well as next to any open flame spot; there must be carbon monoxide alarms fitted next to any internal gas burning equipment; any gas water heaters must be serviced regularly by a qualified engineer; gas/electric checks must have the appropriate certificates issued; and the pool depth markings must be clearly indicated in the pool area.

viii) Do make sure that your rental holiday home has public liability insurance cover.

ix) Do make sure that the property is set up with all the essentials for rentals, for example: good access; clear instructions on how to use property equipment, such as the washing machine, dishwasher and other kitchen appliances; modern sized, good quality beds (not the charming old-fashioned Portuguese ones); matching, good quality bed linen and bathroom towels; modern bathrooms; hairdryers; TV with international channels, Wi-Fi; quality garden furniture, etc. Most tour operators will give you a list of what they consider to be the essentials for a successful rental.

x) Do have a professional photographer take pictures of your rental holiday home, as nothing will sell it better than great photographs. These should include some mood shots showing the property set out for holidays, for example: pool loungers, cocktails by the pool, a towel and sun hat on a chair, etc.

xi) Do create a "Villa Welcome Book" to be presented to clients on arrival. This might list any special instructions or warnings, as well as general information regarding local attractions and things to do. This should be updated annually and include the following: contact numbers in case of emergencies; instructions on how to work essential electrical equipment; exact staff duties and hours of work; extra services available on request/payable locally; local map and tourist information; recommended restaurants, beaches, golf courses, etc.

xii) Do choose your management agent carefully and make sure they are efficient with staff timekeeping, cleanliness, maintenance, changeover day turnarounds, payments in and out, etc. A management agent who also does rentals kills two birds with one stone, but the way to increase your occupation rate is to list your property with several rental agents, as well as take the odd private booking yourself from family and friends. Keep your options open and don't sign any exclusivity contracts.

Last but not least, enjoy your time in Portugal – the people, food, wine and sunshine are definitely worth it even if the bureaucracy is a nightmare at times. Remember that there are some excellent professionals out there to help you!

Mandy de Azevedo Coutinho, Lisbon
Founder & Manager of Almond Blossom Villa Rentals
www.almondblossom-rentalvillas.com

Builders and Architects

If you decide to buy directly from a builder or developer, have them build a new house on a plot, or have any work done on the property you are purchasing, such as renovations or extensions, then make some checks. The same applies to using an architect.

Checking Out Your Builder

A builder, who undertakes large renovation works or projects, as opposed to minor repairs, must be a registered builder and should have a building permit *(Alvará de Construção)*. These are renewed annually and can be checked on the *INCI* website.

To check for builders' permits go to *www.inci.pt* and click on *Construção* on the left-hand side followed by *Consulta de Empresas* and then *Alvará*.

You can then insert all or any of the following: building permit Nº *(Alvará)*, individual or company fiscal Nº *(NIF/NIPC)*, company/builder's name *(Denominação)*, postal code *(Código Postal)* or locality *(Localidade)*, before clicking on *Pesquisar* in the bottom right-hand corner.

If you want to find all registered builders in a particular district *(Distrito)* or council area *(Concelho)*, click on the arrows alongside the relevant boxes and highlight the area you want and then click on *Pesquisar.* By clicking on the individual builder you can then check all their details, such as the expiry date of the building permit *(Data de Validade),* their individual or company fiscal N° *(NIF/NIPC),* their address *(Morada),* their telephone number (*Telefone*), when they first registered *(Data de Inscrição)* and the categories *(Categorias/Habilitações)* — i.e. the type and size of works they can carry out. The licence depends on such things, as the type of equipment they have and the number of qualified staff the company has on board.

Builders undertaking more minor works should have a *Título de Registo.* These are valid for five years and then renewed. A builder working under a *Título de Registo* has a limit of €16.600 for his works at the time of writing.

To check if a builder has a *Título de Registo* go to *www.inci.pt* and click on *Construção* on the left-hand side followed by *Consulta de Empresas* and then *Título de Registo.*

Follow the same steps as for searching for a builder's permit *(Alvará)* above. There are many more categories for builders with a *Título de Registo* and you might need some help deciphering them.

If you need to contact *INCI* to make further enquiries or to make a complaint, click on *Contactos* on the home page at the top under the banner.

Remember the complaints book (*livro de reclamações*) mentioned in the *Real Estate Agents & Vendors'* chapter can also be requested for complaints.

If you want to find out if your builder is a limited company, you can check by consulting the *Portal da Empresa* website at *www.portaldaempresa.pt*.

Click on *empresa online* at the top of the page in the banner followed by *Pesquisa de nomes (firmas ou denominações) existentes* under *Pedido de nome* halfway down on the left-hand side. Enter the name of the company that you wish to find where it says *Nome*, and then click on *Pesquisar*. You can also add in the council area (*Concelho*), if you wish to narrow down your search. Click on the company's *NIPC* number to get further information.

If after trying this you still do not find the company you are looking for, you can contact the local commercial registry office *(conservatória do registo comercial)* in the area where the company is situated to double check. At this office, you can also obtain more information on a company, for example directors' names and formation date, etc. You may have to pay a few Euros to obtain this information. To find the address of your local office, go to *www.irn.mj.pt/IRN/sections/irn/contactos* and click on *Conservatórias de registo comercial* under the *Serviços desconcentrados do IRN, I.P.* subheading. You can then download the file. This will give you a list of all the *conservatórias do registo commercial* in Portugal.

Note that electricians and gas fitters in Portugal must also be registered and licensed. Your builder will usually recommend these technicians to you. Utility companies will not certify an installation and make a connection unless it has been fitted by a qualified, registered technician.

Checking Out Your Architect

To make checks on an architect, in order to see that they are correctly registered, go to the *Ordem dos Arquitectos* website at *www.arquitectos.pt* and click on *Para o público* at the top followed by *consulte um arquitecto* and then *encontre um arquitecto* on the left-hand side.

Insert the name of the architect in the box marked *Nome* and then click on *Pesquisar*. If you need to contact the *Ordem dos Arquitectos* to make any further enquiries or a complaint, go to the top right-hand side of the home page and click on *Contactos*.

Note that there are many people in Portugal working as if they are architects when they are, in fact, only a draftsman/woman regulated by the local council *(câmara municipal)*. They need to have their work signed off by a fully qualified architect. Make sure that you know exactly what you are getting for your money. If you want a qualified, graduate architect, then check that they are with their governing body, as detailed above.

You may also need the services of an engineer during the planning and construction stages. The architect will quite often work alongside an engineer, but if you wish to find one yourself or check that they are registered with their professional body, then you can do so via the *Ordem dos Engenheiros* website at *www.ordemengenheiros.pt*.

Click on *Pesquisa de Membros* in the left-hand column and then you can search via name (*Nome*), registered number (*Cédula Profissional*), type of engineering (*Colégio*), region (*Região*), level of qualification (*Nível de Qualificação*) or specialisation (*Especializações*).

If you need to contact the *Ordem dos Engenheiros*, click on *Contactos* in the left-hand column at the bottom.

As of 2008, an engineer must sign off a project, as well as the architect.

Planning Procedure

As mentioned in the *Real Estate Agents & Vendors'* chapter, planning permission in Portugal can take a very long time (from six months to a year), so you should be prepared for a long wait and not try to rush things. It is also never advisable to start any building works without the correct permissions and licences.

Planning permission in Portugal has tightened up considerably over the last few years and as well as facing the possibility of large fines from the local council, you could also now be left with an illegal property, which may be difficult to sell at a later date.

Minor works, maintenance, restoration and repairs that do not alter the façade of a property, as well as internal works that do not alter the structure of a property generally do not need planning permission. However, it is always best to check with the local council (*câmara municipal*) first.

The architect will prepare all the documentation and plans to request a construction licence. He or she should also supervise the work that the builder carries out to make sure that it is completed according to the plans and to the necessary standard, and must sign off the book of works (*Livro de Obra*).

The first stage of planning is called the Architectural Project (*Projecto de Arquitectura*). It is a comprehensive brief including architectural drawings, a topographical survey and a list of the materials to be used. This is submitted to the local council first for approval.

The second stage is called the Specialities Project (*Projecto de Especialidades*). This part of the project covers the engineering required to complete the build, e.g. information on structure and stability, sewerage, water, acoustics, electricity, ventilation, etc. and is usually compiled in conjunction with an engineer.

Once both the *Projecto de Arquitectura* and *Projecto de Especialidades* have been approved, your chosen builder (with his building permit and proof of insurance cover) can then obtain the building licence (*licença de construção*) from the local council. They will also issue the builder with a notice (*aviso*) to be displayed outside the construction site showing that they have permission to build.

When the property has been completed, the builder must arrange for an inspection (*vistória*) by the local council. This request must also be accompanied by a declaration from the supervising architect or engineer that the building has been constructed according to the plans and building regulations. This person should be someone registered with the local council with legal permission to make such declarations.

Note that the local council can also make inspections at any point during the works, if they so choose.

Changes to the regulations in March 2008 now mean that a local council inspection may not always be required, unless the architect or engineer does not take full responsibility for the works.

A habitation licence *(licença de habitação)* will then be issued if all is correct.

The final payment to your builder should not be made until you have received the habitation licence.

As of March 30th 2004 a builder now also needs to produce a *ficha técnica de habitação* (*FTH*). See the *Habitation Licence, Pre-1951 Certificate and Ficha Técnica de Habitação* section of the *What's What* chapter.

The property must then be registered at the local tax office *(serviço das finanças)* and land registry *(conservatória do registo predial)*.

The builder should also supply you with a five-year warranty against any structural defects. Make sure that you get this warranty in writing. However, remember that this does not exclude you from getting your own structural property insurance.

Recommendations

When seeking an architect or builder, get independent recommendations and references from other people and go to see some of their previous work. A local builder may also be preferable to one from a different part of the country.

There are plenty of forums on the Internet now for Portugal, so this can be another means of swapping information and recommendations. The same method could be used for real estate agents and legal representatives.

Be aware that a real estate agent might be on commission from a builder and/or architect, so they aren't necessarily the best people to ask to make a recommendation. It is also a good idea to use an architect who is independent from the builder.

Translation and Supervision

Make sure you are precise about everything you want done and include everything. Don't be vague and don't make assumptions. If there are any doubts due to language difficulties then use an independent translator.

If you are not going to be around to supervise the work then you may need to consider having someone do this on your behalf, or to employ a project manager. As with everything else involved in buying a property in Portugal, don't cut corners and try to save a little bit on the expense. You may find that it will land you in deeper financial problems further down the line.

It is a good idea to get a Portuguese-speaking friend or Portuguese translator to go with you to check each stage at the local council *(câmara municipal)*. You should be able to inspect any planning file, although sometimes you have to request the file a day in advance, which enables you to make sure that what your builder/architect is telling you is true and that you are not being fobbed off.

Buying From a Builder and Building Contracts

Buying a plot of land from a builder and then having him also do the work is not always a good idea.

Compare the prices of similar plots in the area, as well as the building costs with other builders.

If you do decide to go ahead with the same builder then make sure that you have two contracts drawn up, one for the land and one for the building, and get the land deed title sorted out first before doing the building contract.

Check also that the builder actually owns the land he is selling and if not, who does? It is obviously the owner's name that must appear on the deed *(escritura)*.

Buying off-plan has been a popular means of buying property in Portugal for many years, but it can have its drawbacks. If a builder goes bankrupt then your property could remain unfinished, or while your property might have been completed, it could end up sitting on an unfinished development.

It is wise to check if your builder has an insurance policy, which will protect you in the event that the company goes bust. It isn't unusual to be asked for an amount of money to act as a small holding deposit, in order to reserve a property before the promissory contract *(contrato de promessa de compra e venda)* is signed. Obviously this should be well documented and invoiced.

For buying off-plan or employing a builder to build a property on a plot, you should seek the advice of a legal representative in the drawing up of a contract.

The contract should include:

- ❑ The stage payments (which can vary in percentages).
- ❑ Dates for the stage payments.
- ❑ A timetable for completion to tie up with the payments.
- ❑ A date for completion.
- ❑ Penalties for failure to complete on time.
- ❑ Guarantees.
- ❑ Insurance policy against non-completion.
- ❑ A copy of the plans and drawings and any clauses.
- ❑ An amount for a set period of time to act as a guarantee against the builder not addressing any faults.

Make sure that the work to be done at each stage is complete before parting with any money, as the percentage of construction work carried out is more important than just dates and times. Do not give any more money than the contract states at each stage.

In relation to buying off-plan you must also consider that, unlike the UK, there is no leasehold system. Apartments, and occasionally townhouses and some semi-detached properties, are sold under a system of 'horizontal property' *(propriedade horizontal)*. A builder must sign a deed at the notary *(cartório notarial)* in order to create this system and, therefore, set up individual legal titles for each unit. These individual titles are then registered at the land registry *(conservatória do registo predial)* and each is given an individual title number.

The deed of 'horizontal property' should include:

- ❑ Where the units are situated, their divisions and composition.
- ❑ The relative value of each unit in the form of a percentage of the whole building.
- ❑ The authorised use of each unit.
- ❑ The condominium rules and restrictions — including details of the administration and maintenance.
- ❑ What makes up the communal parts.
- ❑ Arbitration rules in the event of any disputes between owners.

Also see the *Condominiums* chapter.

Paying Builders and Architects

When using a builder or architect for any work, regardless of whether it is a small job or not, ask for invoices *(facturas)* for everything. Pay the VAT *(IVA –* currently 23,25%). It may seem 'like getting blood out of a stone' at times — but don't take no for an answer. These invoices may help to reduce your capital gains tax liability if you later want to sell the property. In this regard, they are valid for five years. Remember that trying to save a bit of tax here and there could cost you dearly later.

You might also need proof that they did the work if you ever need to call them back at a later stage because of defective workmanship. Do not pay 'cash in hand' for anything.

Discuss with your bank and/or financial adviser the best way to make any payments to your builder or architect so that your money can be accounted for.

Builders and Legal Advice

It is a bad idea to use a lawyer *(advogado)* or *solicitador(a)* recommended by a builder, or in any way associated to a builder/development company. This can be a recipe for disaster due to vested interests. If you use their legal representative then how will you know if they are acting in *your* best interests and not those of the builder/developer when they draw up the contract? See the chapter on *Professional Legal Advice*.

CASE STUDY: HAZEL DICKSON

I am originally from Edinburgh and my partner and I moved to Portugal in February 2008. I had been coming to Central Portugal for many years, as my mum had moved here. She used to buy and sell properties and we invested in a property together back in 2004. After selling our first property for a profit, we then purchased a house in a little village, which we moved into when we first arrived. Two years on from there, we found another property we wanted to renovate. My husband and I did a lot of the work ourselves and stripped it right back. However, we kept a lot of the original features, for example the beams, stone walls and antique windows. It is a very proud feeling to live in a house that you have designed and worked on with your own blood, sweat and tears.

A lot of people couldn't understand why my partner and I moved to such a rural part of Portugal after living in a big city, as we were very young to be taking such a leap. I am now 32 and my partner is 33. Basically, we were looking to get onto the property market in Edinburgh, which proved very difficult, and we were also in stressful jobs, which we hated. I was the manager of a clothes shop on Princes Street and my partner worked for a bank. So we decided that, as we were young, it was worth the risk and if things didn't work out, we could always go back. Saying that, we are still here after nearly seven years. It is quiet but that's how we like it. Back in the UK, the weekend would come and we'd go out at 10 P.M. and have a few drinks with mates, but here it is much more of a café culture and, as it is so cheap to eat out in most places, people go out for lunches and drinks during the day.

We didn't have a clear-cut plan for work when we moved to Portugal, but took the attitude that we would try our hand at anything. My partner has gone from banking to construction. He now works for a Portuguese builder and is his right-hand man, translator and good friend.

Two years ago we got married here. My husband is Scottish and so I felt the need for all the men to wear kilts, which being that is was hottest day of the year, I am sure they appreciated. It was a great day. However, in hindsight I would have done the legalities in the UK, as the process with the paperwork was painstaking. We almost ended up not having the documents for the day to go ahead, which was stressful to say the least! The cost of doing the paperwork here was also a lot more expensive than in the UK; it cost us over €1000. Luckily, it all worked out well in the end.

Since moving to Portugal, I have discovered a love of gardening, as things grow so easily. I have a vegetable patch and the vegetables taste so much better when they are home grown. The food is much healthier too. In the summertime we live on salads, and in the winter, lots of vegetable soup. You can recreate most English meals with local ingredients and, when you can't, it doesn't matter as you can try the Portuguese food and new recipes. We also have a large bread oven in our garden, in which my partner cooked Christmas dinner last year. In addition, we have about 50 vines, and last year my mum's partner added some to their crop so they could make homemade wine. I think this year we might try making some ourselves; I quite like the idea of trampling grapes with my feet although I don't know how many people will want to drink it after!

The cost of living here is very low. On a monthly basis we spend about half of what we spent in the UK. Food and wine is cheap, though some things do cost more, like cars and electrical equipment. The Portuguese people are lovely. Our neighbours are always giving us fruit from their fruit trees, jams, flowers and so on. The language does take time to learn and you find some people are easier to understand than others, but on the whole people are very accommodating and patient when you are speaking with them. Of course, the more you practise when out and about, the better you become. I always say that our Portuguese improves considerably after a few bottles of *Sagres*!

It was difficult for the first few years, and we do still miss our family and friends, but we have no regrets and absolutely love it here — and our loved ones know where to visit for a holiday.

Hazel Dickson, Arganil

Professional Legal Advice

Foreigners unable to speak Portuguese, or only to a limited degree, often decide to use some form of legal advice when buying property in Portugal and this is usually a very wise decision.

*Note that another form of purchasing property in Portugal now exists called *Casa Pronta* (see the *What's What* chapter), which means that using a notary and signing a final deed is no longer compulsory. However, it is assumed that most foreign purchasers will still wish to use a notary and sign a final deed.

Types of Representative

You may approach either a *solicitador(a)* or an *advogado(a)* for legal representation.

A *solicitador(a)*, despite the similarity of the name to the English solicitor, is not the same. In Portugal, a *solicitador(a)* is more akin to someone who does conveyancing, or a legal executive. They do not have to study for a degree and are not permitted to do court work. They are regulated by the *Câmara dos Solicitadores*.

You can **check whether a *solicitador(a)* is registered with the *Câmara dos Solicitadores*** by going to *www.solicitador.net*.

You can view the site in English as well as Portuguese. Go to the search box on the left-hand side and put in the name of the *Solicitador* you wish to find. You can also search by locality or judicial district. If you click on the name of the *Solicitador*, you will be able to see their full address (*Morada*), telephone numbers (*Telefone*), email address and their registered number (*Cédula*).

For more options, you can click on advanced search and search via things such as: name (*Nome*), town/court area (*Comarca*), address (*Morada*), postal code (*Código Postal*), and registered number (*Cédula*) and then click on *Pesquisar*.

To check for firms of *solicitadores*, go the advanced search section again and highlight *Sociedade* in the *Filtro* box. You can then search using name (*Nome*), address (*Morada*) or postal code (*Código Postal*).

An *advogado(a)*, is the equivalent of a lawyer, barrister or solicitor in the UK. Not all *advogado(a)s* specialise, so you could find a lawyer dealing with a property purchase one day, a divorce the day after and in court defending a criminal the day after that. However, if you want to find a specialist property lawyer, it may well be worth the extra expense.

Lawyers study for five years at university and gain the title *Dr(a)* if they graduate. They are regulated by the *Ordem dos Advogados*.

116

To **check that an** *advogado(a)* **is qualified**, and what their principal practising address and registered Nº *(cédula Nº)* is, go to *www.oa.pt* and click on *Pesquisa de advogados* on the left-hand side.

Put the lawyer's name in the box marked *Nome* and click on the magnifying glass symbol. Their address, telephone/fax numbers, email address and registered Nº should all be listed. If a number of lawyers come up with the same or similar names, then you can narrow down your search by putting in their office address (*Morada*), postcode (*Código Postal*), or town/court area (*Comarca*). You can also search by council district (*Conselho Distrital*) or registered number (*Cédula*), if known. You can list in order of the above categories by clicking on *Ordenar Por*.

Surprisingly, *advogado(a)s* are not obliged to register all their practising addresses, but only a principal office. Lawyers have been found to have one address listed with the *Ordem dos Advogados* and a completely different one in the yellow pages *(páginas amarelas)*. The Portuguese yellow pages can be found in both Portuguese and English (click at the bottom of the page to change language) at *www.pai.pt*.

Many lawyers work together as a firm and you should check on this when employing an individual lawyer.

The *Ordem dos Advogados* website is currently not listing details of firms, but should you wish to check on this you can contact them by telephone. They usually have an

English-speaking operative on their switchboard, if required. Click on *Contactos* on the top bar of the home page for their contact details.

Doing Your Own Checks

In an ideal world using a legal representative should mean that you are protected and that you receive honest and good advice. However, just because someone has a degree, a title and a few initials after their name, it does not guarantee that they will behave in a moral and ethical manner.

It is strongly recommended that you do some of your own checks alongside those of your legal representative. This way you can cross-reference with your legal representative and get clarification for anything that you are not sure about. If you don't speak Portuguese yourself, take an independent Portuguese translator, or reliable Portuguese-speaking friend, to do these checks. Don't cut corners on this because of the extra time or expense. It could cost you considerably more later.

Selecting Your Legal Representative

Many real estate agents, builders and developers will recommend a lawyer or *solicitador(a)* to you. This will more often than not be *their* lawyer or *solicitador(a)*.

It is much better to choose your own independent legal representation. If you don't, you can never be sure that they will be acting in your best interests and not those of the vendor. Get recommendations from other people whenever possible.

It has also been known for a lawyer to act for both vendor and purchaser. This is not permitted and totally unethical. Another practice is to sometimes get a lawyer 'friend' (often working from the same office) to deal with the other party. In effect, the purchase and sale is then still very much 'under one roof'.

Use your common sense when selecting your legal advice and keep a close eye on proceedings. Ask for quotations from a few lawyers/*solicitadores*. On average they charge 1 to 2% of the property purchase value for their legal fees. However, this can be quite variable depending on the area in Portugal and it has been known for some to charge as much as 2.5% and others as little as 0.5%. Remember that going for the cheapest lawyer, in order to try to save money isn't necessarily the best idea.

What You Should Expect

Make sure that they set down exactly what they will be doing via an engagement letter, which should confirm the terms and conditions of how they will be acting on your behalf. Find out, for example, if they are going to be dealing with the change over of contracts for the various utility services as well as the property searches.

Don't proceed without an engagement letter. Make sure that you get every step clarified in writing from your legal representative. Except for routine matters, try to insist on receiving hard copies on their official headed stationery rather than emails.

Check with the *Ordem dos Advogados* if a lawyer is an individual or an associate in a firm of lawyers, as detailed above, and is, therefore, using the right headed stationery.

You should also insist on an invoice *(factura)* for any money you pay to your legal representative on proper-headed stationery, which should also show their fiscal number (*número de contribuinte* or *NIF*), together with a 'narrative' itemising everything that they have done on your behalf.

Remember, that as well as the legal fees, you will also have to pay:

- ❑ Notary fees.
- ❑ Deed (*escritura*) registration fees.
- ❑ Stamp duty (0.8%).
- ❑ Purchase tax (*imposto municipal sobre transmissôes onerosas de imóveis — IMT*).

See the Appendix for the 2015 *IMT* rates.

Always get a detailed breakdown of these costs for your individual circumstances, so that there are no unexpected expenses. Speak to your legal representative and a financial adviser about this.

See the Appendix for a Purchase Budget Calculator.

Remember, it is also not permitted for your legal representative to make money on your money in his/her client account. So make sure that you get a firm date at the notary to sign the final deed and transfer the money to coincide with this date.

Why let your money sit in someone else's account while waiting for a convenient slot at the notary to finalise your purchase, or while you are waiting for your legal representative to complete his/her enquiries?

Another way of paying for your property could be by a form of banker's draft *(cheque visado)* direct from a Portuguese bank account, which you can easily set up. You can then hand this cheque over to the vendors on the day of the final deed signing, without having to put your money through anyone else's account. Check with your bank and/or financial adviser about the best method of payment for you.

Finally, make sure you are legitimate yourself. Don't be sweet talked into trying to evade tax or anything else untoward. You may find that if you have a problem further down the line people could use this against you to stop you going to the authorities and you could end up a lot worse off.

Promissory Contract

If you decide to pay a deposit (usually 10%) to hold the property and sign a promissory contract *(contrato de promessa de compra e venda)* then make sure that it is checked over or drawn up by a legal representative. Doing this ensures that any clauses you wish to be included are written into the contract. If you withdraw from the sale then you will lose your deposit. If the vendor withdraws then they will have to pay you double.

It is important that you know exactly what you are agreeing to, so get a translation in English and have both the Portuguese and English versions checked by an independent translator to make sure that they are identical.

Never sign anything without being entirely sure what you are agreeing to. You can go straight to the final deed stage without a promissory contract, but when paying a deposit it is usually advisable to get one.

This contract should include:

- ❑ The names, addresses, civil states, nationalities (if non-Portuguese), birthplaces, ID Nᵒs (ID card/*bilhete de identidade*, residence card or passport) and fiscal numbers (*números de contribuinte/NIF*) of both parties.
- ❑ Details and location of the property.
- ❑ Land registry certificate Nᵒ (*certidão de registo predial/teor Nᵒ*).
- ❑ Tax office document Nᵒs (*caderneta Nᵒs*).
- ❑ The amount of deposit paid.
- ❑ The agreed purchase price.
- ❑ The agreed date for the final deed signing.

- ❑ Habitation licence (*licença de habitação*) or pre-1951 certificate (*pre-1951 certidão*).
- ❑ *Ficha técnica de habitação* for post March 30th 2004 properties.
- ❑ Land registry certificate (*certidão de registo predial/teor*).
- ❑ Tax office document(s) for rustic/urban property (*caderneta(s) urbana/rústica*).
- ❑ Energy efficiency certificate (*certificado energético da habitação*).

If there is a mortgage involved, the contract will be drawn up by the bank and signed at the notary office. Before this stage, your legal representative will provisionally register the mortgage at the land registry (*conservatória do registo predial*), which includes the amount of the mortgage. Details of this should also be included on the deed and an official from the bank should be in attendance to sign.

If it is a company selling the property, then a *certidão de registo commercial* should be provided showing the partners and shareholders, who has what powers, and the business details, address, etc. ID and fiscal Nºs for the owner/partners also need to be provided as well as a power of attorney for the person signing on behalf of the company.

If at all possible, request a copy of the final deed and an English translation a few days before signing. You can then check it through with a translator and take it with you to crosscheck with what you are signing on the day. You can also check that the correct identities for those involved are detailed.

If, at any time, you are not clear or you are unhappy about what is going on then don't feel embarrassed to halt proceedings to clarify anything you wish. The values on the deed will usually be in text only and not numerals, so as yet another safeguard, find out how the amount is written in Portuguese and write it down to take with you.

With regard to making sure that the correct price for the property you are buying goes on the deed, it is not advisable to agree with the vendor to 'under declare' the property value and pay part of the price in cash 'under the table'.

Not only is this practice strictly illegal but it also leaves you liable for a heavy fine if discovered by the tax office.

Paying less purchase tax due to this deception might seem a good idea at the time, but it will almost certainly result in a larger capital gains tax bill, if and when you decide to sell the property.

If you are buying a 'mixed' property, that is, a property with both a rustic and urban *caderneta* (see the *Tax Office – Serviço das Finanças* section of the *What's What* chapter for information regarding *cadernetas*) then check how the price is to be divided up between the rustic part and the urban part.

Buildings obviously have a far greater value than rustic land and in general the ratio is 10% on the land and 90% on the house but get reputable financial advice if you have any doubts in this area. Also note that these days all properties are revalued by the tax office after a purchase has taken place.

If there are any fixtures and fittings involved in the sale of the property then these should be dealt with separately and are independent of the price of the property.

What You Should Receive

Make sure that your legal representative gives you proper authenticated (with a stamp/seal) copies of all documents, such as:

- ❑ Promissory contract.
- ❑ Final deed.
- ❑ Land registry certificate.
- ❑ Purchase tax (*IMT*) invoice.
- ❑ Habitation licence or pre-1951 certificate.
- ❑ *Ficha técnica de habitação* for post-30th March 2004 properties.
- ❑ *Cadernetas* (these should have your name and tax number on now and not the previous owners).
- ❑ Energy efficiency certificate.

Make sure that your property is registered at the land registry *(conservatória do registo predial)* as soon as possible after the final deed has been signed. **This is very important.**

Complaints

If you find yourself in the unfortunate position of having to make a complaint against your *solicitador(a)* or lawyer then you can do so by writing to their relevant governing bodies.

For lawyers go to the *Ordem dos Advogados* website at *www.oa.pt* and click on *Contactos* on the top bar.

For *solicitadores* go to the *Câmara dos Solicitadores* website at *www.solicitador.net* and click on *Contacte-nos* (Contact Us) in the top right-hand corner or *Contactos* on the main top bar.

CASE STUDY: ANDREW PENDLEBURY

I was born and spent my first few years in a small Lancashire village where my father worked as a design technology teacher and my mother stayed at home to bring up my sister and I. My father was always looking for other opportunities, both locally and internationally, and one day he applied for a teaching position at an international school in Portugal. He was accepted and so we found ourselves packing up our belongings, colour coding each individual toy, depending on whether it was coming or staying (at the age of five *all* of my toys were coming), and making the two-and-a-half-hour flight to Lisbon.

St Julian's, the international school where my father obtained a position (and eventually my mother too), also became our school. It is situated in Carcavelos, a small beachside town 20 minutes along the *Linha de Cascais* from Lisbon, so it is close enough to the hustle and bustle of city life but also far enough away to feel like a calm beach resort.

Although we went to school in Carcavelos, we ended up living just a little further along the coast near Cascais, a quaint, scenic town with a fair sized international community. With its plentiful beaches, safe environment, and sporting and outdoor lifestyle, it was the perfect location for young children.

At St Julian's School I followed the International Baccalaureate programme, which while challenging seemed to be a good scheme, and I soon became bilingual. My friends were a mixture of Portuguese and international and outside of school my time was spent hitting the local beaches and going out into town over the weekend. There's nothing like a beach bar with a coastal view while sipping on a Caipirinha! A 15-minute walk to the centre of Cascais also meant that I never needed to worry about getting home late at night.

After completing my studies at St Julian's, I took a gap year and worked there as a carpenter (making benches from felled trees) before returning to the UK to start a degree course at the University of Brighton. Over the next few years, I travelled back and forth doing a number of different things, partly due to suffering with glandular fever (which interrupted my course for a year) and partly because the job market was rather difficult in Portugal. However, on meeting my wife, Sarah, who is Portuguese, I decided to move back to Cascais permanently and settle down.

Three kids later, we still wonder where the time has gone. If you have children, Portugal *is* the place to bring them up. No one groans at you on planes when they are noisy and you always seem to get some elderly lady come up and interact with them, which always puts a smile on their faces. In general, the Portuguese are polite and very child friendly. However, the politeness stops in cars. *Don't* expect them to stop if you are on a zebra crossing - *they won't*!

Another great attribute about living in Portugal is the food. Come off the main roads onto the side streets and you will often find yourself at some fantastic Portuguese restaurant. They will be nothing to write home about when you walk in, but the quality, quantity and the price of the food will be second to none. You always end up eating slightly too much, which you come to regret when you can't fit in the *mousse de chocolate* or *baba de camelo* at the end.

An additional positive to Portugal is its public transport, which is extremely cheap compared to the UK. For example, a typical 45-minute train journey from Cascais to the centre of Lisbon costs less than €3 and the inter-city trains (*Alfa Pendular/intercidade*) are fast, comfortable and, somewhat surprisingly, on time.

Unfortunately, working in Portugal is where the fairy tale ends. Generally speaking pay is very low (I was once offered a telesales job for a whopping €1,25 per hour!), and businesses tend to take advantage of the fact that people need work, and as a result, offer very poor packages. They know there is always someone who will accept. Fortunately, all the work that I have carried out has been with international organisations, and I was even lucky enough to work remotely for a while as a designer for my former British employer.

A drawback to working as a self-employed person is that you have to use what is known as "green receipts" (*recibos verdes*). You are required to fill out these receipts and hand them to your employer each month or whenever your role is complete. In order to obtain a booklet of them and 'open' your self-employment, you have to spend a morning queuing at the local *finanças* office and pay a small fee. When your job is finished, you must then go back again and 'close' them. You have to do this for each different job role or service you offer. To this day, I still don't really know how to fill them out!

Paperwork in Portugal is never ending. It is slowly getting better with more services now available online, but be prepared to fill in lots of forms with lots of different people. There seems to be a great lack of communication between the various departments and getting a simple or straightforward answer is rarely easy.

After 12 years of renting, my parents decided to buy their first property and settled on a new build. The process wasn't too difficult although the bank requested a guarantor when applying for the mortgage. However, within the first few years, cracks started to appear in the living room wall and the constructor wasn't too keen to pay for any of the work required. It has to be said that at the time (and perhaps still now) it seemed that the constructors went in for cheaper quality fittings while trying to make the build *look* expensive.

Their second property purchase was a rural one and although for the most part it went well, there was a five-hour delay before the final deed could be signed while they had to wait for one more document to be collected. A strong celebratory whisky made up for the wait though!

My wife bought her first property in Cascais, and the purchasing and signing were relatively simple. However, my tip would be to always get a *solicitador* or lawyer (*advogado*) on board for any property purchases. Houses are often passed down from generation to generation and frequently the paperwork gets misplaced or lost. This can lead to unforeseen payments and fines!

We are now looking to purchase a project house inland to keep ourselves busy. Once you come out of the city centre it can be very cheap, and if you are happy to live right out in the countryside, you can often find a bargain. However, you would probably have to be prepared to do some major renovation (if not reconstruction) works. It is well worth talking to the locals, as they will know the ins and outs of the area best. They may also be able to recommend reliable, local tradespeople to use.

Andrew Pendlebury, Cascais
www.theforefootrunner.com
www.perfectdesignbits.com
www.tinyhandsandfeet.com

Mortgages and Offshore Buyers

In the past, trying to obtain a mortgage in Portugal (especially if you were a foreigner) was extremely difficult. However, things have moved on and there now seem to be many banks and mortgage companies offering loans to purchase property in Portugal.

This said, it should be noted that due to the amount of bad credit in Portugal and the recent recession Portuguese banks do tend to be a little conservative in their attitude and have quite a low tolerance of risk.

It also seems that some banks are now less likely to loan money to non-resident foreigners, as opposed to resident ones. However, each bank has its own particular likes and dislikes regarding many factors and situations.

So, is it better to obtain your loan in the UK or Portugal? The answer probably depends on the interest rates and where you are receiving your income or where your money is kept.

Getting a mortgage in the same currency as your income could be a good idea, as then you won't have to worry about fluctuations in exchange rates and the payment amounts going up and down each month.

If you obtain a Portuguese mortgage and your money is mostly in the UK then you will have to consider the likely costs involved in transferring it. If you have most of your money in Portugal, however, or are working there, then this will not be an issue.

Interest rates on a Euro mortgage obtained in the UK, are likely to be similar to those of a Portuguese mortgage, as most financial matters in Europe are connected to the Euribor and the interbank lending rate — *www.euribor-rates.eu.*

Whatever your situation seek reputable, qualified and independent financial advice before making a commitment to any loan — be it in the UK or Portugal.

Everyone's financial situation is different and while one can read general advice here and in other books, your circumstances are unique to you. The financial adviser should also preferably be someone who knows about Portuguese Law.

You will have to show that you are in a strong financial position to gain approval and it can also take a long time to arrange, possibly up to three months! Although it has been known for people to obtain approval within a couple of weeks.

The first bank to arrange mortgage loans to British citizens, which could be secured on the property in Portugal, as opposed to a house in the UK, was Banco Totta, now Banco Santander Totta, in London. They started a specialist mortgage scheme in 1987 and are still one of the market leaders in this field. Other banks have since joined them.

Here is a list of some Portuguese banks offering mortgages:

- Millennium BCP: *www.millenniumbcp.pt*
- Novo Banco: *www.novobanco.pt*
- Banif: *www.banif.pt*
- Barclays: *www.barclays.pt*
- Santander Totta: *www.santandertotta.co.uk*
- Caixa Geral de Depósitos: *www.cgd.pt*
- Banco Português de Investimento: *www.bancobpi.pt*
- Banco Bilbao e Vizcaya: *www.bbva.pt*

Most of these sites have the option to view in English. Just look for an English flag, international clients or "EN" on the homepage. Many also have a mortgage simulator.

The maximum loan to value (LTV) varies from 60% to 80% of the valuation or purchase price of the property. It is usually for a period of up to 30 years, if non-resident, and up to 50 years, if resident, and must be completed by the age of 70 or 75. A minimum loan can be anywhere between €50,000 and €150,000 depending on the lender.

There is generally a penalty for early repayment although some overpayments may be allowed. The variable rate penalty is 0.50% and the fixed rate, 2% for the fixed rate period, reverting to 0.50% subsequently.

The fixed rate is linked to either a three or six-month Euribor rate and increased by the margin (spread) that the bank applies.

Many banks and mortgage companies will recommend, or even insist, that life assurance is taken out — so that must also be considered in your costs, as well as the arrangement and valuation fees. Medical examinations are also usually required. These may be carried out in the UK or Portugal.

As well as lending money for a new build or resale property some banks will also consider loaning money for off-plan stage payments.

The documents required in order to obtain a mortgage in Portugal are much the same as in the UK and other parts of Europe. These generally are:

- ❑ Pay slips and employer reference, if employed.
- ❑ Proof of income, if self-employed, or obtaining another source of income.
- ❑ Tax returns (P60 or equivalent).
- ❑ At least three months' bank statements and bank references.
- ❑ Certified copies of ID cards/passport.
- ❑ Fiscal/tax number.
- ❑ Utility bills.
- ❑ Property documents.

Due to the recent recession, the banks have a lot of repossession properties on their books. Not only might you pick up a bargain by going this route, but you might also find it a lot easier to obtain a mortgage.

In 2003 the Portuguese government 'blacklisted' certain places, like Gibraltar, for offshore property ownership. This led to a lot of people taking their money elsewhere and many with property in those places were led through an expensive maze, which either meant they moved their company to a 'non-blacklisted' place like Delaware or Malta, or bought back their property onshore and paid the taxes.

There was a lot of wild speculation at the time and many people took advantage of the situation by charging fees to give advice and deal with people's affairs. Many people were panicked into making a decision to buy back their properties in their names and pay their dues.

The Portuguese government realised some time later that this had had a negative affect on the property market and therefore reduced the penal tax rates they had imposed on offshore ownership.

For current *IMT* (purchase tax) rates, go to the table in the appendix. The *IMI* (council tax) rate at the time of writing is 1% of the rateable value for property owned by companies in 'blacklisted' jurisdictions (other *IMI* rates are discussed in the next chapter in the *Tax Office – Serviço das Finanças* section).

Remember that an offshore company requires a fiscal representative, even if you are resident in Portugal, and you may have to pay additional fees if you rent out the property, such as when making an annual return, as well as for the general running of the company. Properties owned by companies in 'blacklisted' jurisdictions have to make an annual return regardless of whether they are rented out or not.

Buying a property owned by a company in a 'whitelisted' jurisdiction or from a Portuguese nominee company may give you various tax advantages. However, this is very much dependent on your personal circumstances, so as with anything else financial, seek expert, qualified advice before making a decision.

If you decide to go down this route, you will usually simply be buying the shares in the company that has the property listed as an asset and so it is recommended that you employ a lawyer knowledgeable in this field to draw up the Share Purchase Agreement.

What's What

As mentioned in the *Real Estate Agents & Vendors'* chapter, if you use a real estate agent in Portugal then copies of most of the following documents listed in this chapter should be in their possession. You should feel free to ask the agent or vendor for any copies if you have an interest in purchasing a property.

In addition, it may well be advisable to collect your own as a safeguard. Your legal representative should also be able to supply copies at your request.

Land Registry – Conservatória do Registo Predial

The land registry *(conservatória do registo predial)* is where you can obtain copies of land registry certificates *(certidões de registo predial,* also known as *certidões de teor).* A land registry certificate will give you important information about the property you are interested in purchasing. It will tell you:

- ❑ Who the current owners are.
- ❑ Who has owned it previously.
- ❑ Whether there are any charges against the property, such as a mortgage *(hipoteca).*
- ❑ Whether there are any special conditions or rights on the property.

- ❏ The number of rooms, and what their functions are.
- ❏ The size of the constructed area and that of the total plot.

This certificate is a crucial document and should mirror the information contained in the *caderneta(s)* (see the *Tax Office — Serviço das Finanças* section in this chapter).

A deed *(escritura)* cannot be signed without a current (less than six months old) copy of this document.

The land registry certificate is also required for carrying out other property related matters, for example when seeking planning consent.

Visit the land registry in the area you are buying the property. To find the address go to *www.irn.mj.pt/IRN/sections/irn/contactos* and click on *Conservatórias de registo predial* under the *Serviços desconcentrados do IRN, I.P.* subheading. You can then download the file. This will give you a list of all the *conservatórias do registo predial* in Portugal.

You will need to know the title number *(certidão Nº)* of the property, or at least the plot number of the land, to gain information.

Ask the person selling you the property for these details if you don't know them.

You can usually ask for either a simple copy *(uma cópia simples)* of the land registry certificate or an authenticated copy *(uma cópia autenticada)*. Simple copies are usually just a few Euros and are useful for initial enquiries. The authenticated copy, which costs considerably more, will have a cover and each page should be stamped with a seal.

Land registry certificates can also be requested online via *www.predialonline.pt* and paid for either by Visa card or at a *multibanco* (Portuguese ATM) using a reference code. However, you will need to have a fairly good grasp of Portuguese to be able to use this website.

The advantage of obtaining an online version is that the registration is valid for six months. Therefore, if any changes are made during those six months, such as a sale, mortgage, succession, etc, this will be reflected online.

If you use a legal representative then he/she should provide you with an authenticated copy after purchase. Your purchase should be registered as soon as possible at the land registry after the final deed or property transfer contract has been signed. It is not until this has been carried out that you actually become the legal owner and is mandatory in Portugal.

If you use the *Casa Pronta* service (see the *Casa Pronta* section) then this is carried out automatically.

NATIVE'S TIP

It is advisable to visit the land registry on the day of completion (preferably with your legal representative, as they will usually be seen to more rapidly) to make one final check on any outstanding debts or for any new entries, which might affect your purchase.

Notary — Cartório Notarial

Until Decree-Law 116/2008 in July 2008 the notary *(cartório notarial)* was the only place where you could complete a property transfer by signing a final deed *(escritura)*. However, since this time final deeds are no longer compulsory and lawyers *(advogados)* or *solicitadores* are also now permitted to authenticate a property transfer and to verify the tax payment.

In addition, property acquisition and the transfer of ownership can all be dealt with at a one-stop shop called *Casa Pronta* (see the next section).

Despite this change in Portuguese law, it is still worth checking to see if the current property owner has a deed and trying to get hold of a copy, as well as obtaining the land registry certificate *(certidão de registo predial/teor)*, in order to confirm that they are, in fact, the owner.

Although a person is likely to sign a deed at the notary closest to the property they are buying this isn't always the case. In fact, a person can sign a deed at any notary in Portugal. If a legal representative cannot find a slot at the nearest notary he/she might call all the others in the area to see which ones have available dates. They might also liaise with the legal representative on the other side (if there is one) to go to the notary most convenient for both of them.

You should be able to find out if, when and where previous deeds were signed by asking at the nearest land registry *(conservatória do registo predial)* to the property (see the previous section).

To find out where a particular notary is situated go to *www.irn.mj.pt/IRN/sections/irn/contactos* and click on *Cartórios Notariais* under the *Serviços desconcentrados do IRN, I.P.* subheading. You can then download the two files. This will give you a list of all the public *(Públicos)* and private *(Privados)* notaries in Portugal.

A few years ago, many notaries became private, which meant that the prices to get copies of deeds and other notarised documents increased substantially.

A deed should be filed under the owner's name (or a company name in the case of offshore owners and Portuguese holding companies).

Knowing the date that the current owner bought the property will also help to locate it in the event that they have records of more than one deed in that name.

The deed will state the declared price of the property and the purchase tax *(IMT)* document number. A copy of this tax document is kept in the file with the deed and will show when it was paid. You can also get a copy of this from the local tax office *(serviço das finanças)*.

Upon signing a final deed, details of the purchase tax paid and copies of the following must be presented: *certidão de registo predial/teor* (less than six months old), the *caderneta(s)* (less than one year old), either a habitation licence *(licença de habitação)* or a pre-1951 certificate *(pre-1951 certidão)*, a *ficha técnica de habitação* (for properties built after March 30th 2004) and an energy efficiency certificate (*certificado energético da habitação*).

Fiscal numbers *(números de contribuinte/NIF)* and identification documents (passport, residence card or ID card numbers and details) also have to be provided.

If you use a legal representative and complete a deed then he/she should provide you with an authenticated copy soon after purchase. You should also be furnished with a copy of the purchase tax document.

The final deed is usually signed between one to three months after signing the promissory contract *(contrato de promessa de compra e venda)*. All the parties involved must agree this date. See the *Professional Legal Advice* chapter for more details on what should appear on both the promissory contract and the final deed, and for more information on power of attorney.

The notary's *(notário(a))* job is to check that all the documentation is present, that the purchase tax has been paid, to read the deed out loud to all those present and to witness the signing after all the parties have agreed that they have understood and accepted the terms of the document.

If you do not understand Portuguese, you will be required to provide a translator. Your legal representative can carry out this function, if they speak English, but it is often a good idea to use a qualified, independent translator.

NATIVE'S TIP

It is wise to check the property before signing the final deed, as you buy it in that condition, and not in the condition as when you first saw it and signed the promissory contract. Check that the vendor hasn't taken anything that you were expecting to be left, or replaced fixed units, such as kitchen and bathroom equipment, with inferior quality ones. Do not go through with the sale unless you are completely satisfied, as it will be extremely difficult to seek any redress later.

Check with your legal representative on your rights if you have any doubts before proceeding.

Casa Pronta

Over the last few years the Portuguese government has been trying to simplify and cut down on its overbearing bureaucracy, as well as reduce costs, under a programme called SIMPLEX. There have been various reforms and initiatives introduced, a notable one being a service called *Casa Pronta – www.casapronta.pt*.

Casa Pronta (literally — 'Ready House') is a one-stop

shop that allows people to do everything related to the buying and selling of property at a single counter in the land registry office (*conservatória do registo predial*). For example: payment of the taxes involved, contracts for buying and selling, *IMI* exemption requests and other necessary registrations. You can use this service whether you need bank credit or not.

To find the nearest land registry office offering this service, you can consult a list at *www.casapronta.pt/CasaPronta/conteudos/postos_atendimen to.jsp*.

The public employee dealing with the property transfer will make the same checks as the notary in terms of the identification of the parties involved and the property documentation.

While this initiative may interest some, especially those with a strong grasp of the Portuguese language, it is probably still advisable for foreign buyers to seek the services of a legal representative and to use the more traditional route involving a notary.

Tax Office — Serviço das Finanças

The local tax office (*serviço das finanças*) is where you obtain your fiscal number (*número de identificação fiscal or NIF*), also known as *número do contribuinte*, in order to open a bank account and buy property in Portugal.

You will need to take ID, a passport for example, and your details will then be entered onto a computer database along with those of your fiscal representative, if required. An A4 sheet showing these details and your fiscal number will then be printed out and given to you.

You should memorise this number or carry it with you at all times, as you will be surprised at how many times you will be asked for this number when doing various things in Portugal.

In the past, it was necessary for a non-resident in Portugal to appoint a fiscal representative to go along with them and sign that they are responsible for any payments/debts in Portugal and to make sure that any tax and financial obligations were met. In May 2011 the EU ruled that this was a violation of the rights of free circulation of people and capital and so this is no longer a requirement for anyone with a permanent address within the EU.

However, individuals and companies with a permanent residence outside of the EU still require a fiscal representative.

A fiscal representative could be anyone in theory but is usually a legal representative, financial adviser or accountant, as the responsibilities are quite onerous. There are also companies that will provide this service.

The local tax office is also the place where you can obtain copies of *cadernetas*. *Caderneta* literally means 'exercise book' but in relation to property it is like a 'log book' showing details of the property and its rateable value. The full title of this document is *caderneta predial*.

There are two types of *caderneta predial*: urban *(urbana)* and rustic *(rústica)*. If you buy a house on a plot in an urbanisation, then you will only have a *caderneta urbana* whereas if you buy a house with land in the countryside, you should have both. It is known as a mixed property *(prédio misto)*. They will give a detailed description of the property.

The urban *caderneta* will show such information as:

❏ Identification *(identificação do prédio)* and localisation *(localização do prédio)* of the property — district *(distrito)*, council *(concelho)* and parish *(freguesia)* — as well as the street name and urbanisation or locale.

❏ Article number *(artigo matricial)*.

❏ The neighbours *(confrontações)*.

❏ A description of the property *(descrição do prédio)* — the number of rooms in the property and what they consist of.

❏ The rateable value of the property *(valor patrimonial)*.

❏ The land and property measurements *(áreas)*.

❏ The owner's name *(nome)*, address for correspondence *(morada)* and fiscal number *(identificação fiscal)*.

The rustic *caderneta* will show such information as:

❏ Identification *(identificação do prédio)* and localisation *(localização do prédio)* of the property -

district (*distrito*), council (*concelho*) and parish (*freguesia*) – as well as the village or locale.

❏ Map section (*secção*) letter(s) and article number (*artigo matricial Nº*).

❏ Land measurements (*áreas*).

❏ How the parcels (*parcelas*) are divided up and the types of tree culture on the land.

❏ The rateable value of the property (*valor patrimonial*).

❏ The owner's name (*nome*), address for correspondence (*morada*) and fiscal number (*identificação fiscal*).

❏ Any alterations (under *observações*) to the land size, e.g. detachments or annexations.

❏ A map should also be attached showing the neighbours and boundaries.

Ask the owner, real estate agent or legal representative for copies before proceeding with a purchase in order that you can see exactly what is on them.

Check whether the details on the *caderneta(s)* are consistent with the land registry certificate *(certidão de registo predial/teor)*. They should be. A final deed (*escritura*) cannot be signed without current (less than one year old) copies of this document.

Once a homeowner, you can also obtain copies of *cadernetas* online at the *Portal das Finanças* website. Go to *www.portaldasfinancas.gov.pt* and click on *Serviços Tributários* and then on *Serviços Tributários* once again on the left-hand side followed by *Consultar*. Scroll down to *Imovéis* in the list and click on *Património Predial*.

In order to register to use the site, go to *Novo Utilizador* in the right-hand column. Fill in your details, i.e. fiscal number (*Nº Contribuinte*), email, telephone (*Telefone*), fiscal address (*Morada Fiscal*) and a security question (*Pergunta*) and answer (*Resposta*). Submit by clicking on *Pedir Senha* at the bottom. You will then be sent a password in the mail to your fiscal address in Portugal (which could be that of your fiscal representative if you have one).

One other matter that may concern you in relation to this department and your property purchase is the possibility of obtaining an exemption from paying your rates (*imposto municipal sobre imóveis — IMI*) once you have completed. This only applies to those who will be resident in Portugal and using the property as their principal residence. You may want to ask your legal representative to carry this out as part of their purchasing duties on your behalf. It should be done within 60 days of purchase.

You can also now request this online at the above website by going to *Serviços Tributários* and then on *Serviços Tributários* again on the left hand side, followed by *Entregar, Declarações, IMI* and *Pedido de Isenção*.

If you use *Casa Pronta,* then this service will be available at the time of the transfer of ownership.

The *IMI* registration value is determined by means of a valuation (*valor patrimonial*) based on the type of property. The following rates are then applied:

- ❑ Urban – 0.3% to 0.5%
- ❑ Rural – 0.8%

Payment is made as follows:

- ❑ <€250 – annually in April
- ❑ €250 to €500 – two payments: April & November
- ❑ >€500 – three payments: April, July & November

At the time of writing, those with a property *valor patrimonial* of up to €125,000 and a taxable income of less than €153,300 in the year previous to the property acquisition will be given a three-year exemption.

Documents needed to obtain this exemption include:

- ❑ Fiscal Nº.
- ❑ Deed (*escritura*).
- ❑ Residency certificate/card.
- ❑ Request form.

Companies acquiring real estate, which constitutes a legal investment, may also benefit from an *IMI* exemption of up to five years.

NATIVE'S TIP

While citizens with a permanent EU residence no longer need to appoint a fiscal representative to be responsible for their financial affairs in Portugal, it may still be worth employing one in order to keep on top of all financial affairs. Tax office notifications often need a reply within 10 to 30 days and will naturally be in Portuguese, so it may make sense to have someone on the ground as a safeguard.

A fiscal representative can supply a full service or merely forward you the bills to pay yourself via Internet banking or direct debit.

Habitation Licence, Pre-1951 Certificate and Ficha Técnica de Habitação

Before purchasing any property, the seller must provide you with either a habitation licence *(licença de habitação)* or a pre-1951 certificate *(pre-1951 certidão)*.

Without one of these documents, you cannot legally buy the property and live in it. You can obtain copies of these at the local council *(câmara municipal)*.

You may also see the term utilisation licence *(licença de utilização)*. Although they are sometimes used interchangeably, the habitation licence usually refers to a building suitable for habitation whereas the utilisation licence refers to buildings for other uses, such as shops.

The builder or responsible architect will ask the local council for a habitation licence when a property construction has been completed. The council will then usually make an inspection known as a *vistória*. If the building has been completed to the correct specifications and building regulations, then a habitation licence is issued (also see the *Builders & Architects'* chapter).

A pre-1951 certificate proves that the building was constructed before August 7th 1951 and, therefore, does not require a habitation licence. Pre-1951 properties that have had work done to them *will* require a habitation licence (and more recently a *ficha técnica de habitação*).

To obtain a pre-1951 certificate the owner has to provide the following to the local council:

- ❏ A set of topographical plans.
- ❏ Photographs.
- ❏ Property documents.
- ❏ Statement of two local witnesses.

If you buy an old property with a pre-1951 certificate and then carry out works to renovate it after gaining building permission, you will need to apply for a habitation licence when the works are completed. You or your builder or architect must apply for this at the local council.

Properties built after March 30th 2004 now also need a *ficha técnica de habitação* (*FTH*). This gives detailed technical information on the property in terms of construction type and the suppliers and materials used. It has been referred to as a building's 'ID card'.

The builder must supply this document to the local council and it must be presented to the notary by the seller or real estate agent at the time of the final deed signing. The seller or real estate agent should also provide you with a copy on request. You can get copies of this document at the local council.

Utilities

One of the most important things you will need to know is how the property you intend to buy gets its water.

Is it from the local council *(câmara municipal)*, or does it have its own borehole *(furo)*, or well *(poço)*? Do you have to buy your supply from a neighbour, or does the local fire service *(bombeiros)* deliver it to a water tank *(cisterna)* on the property?

Without some form of water supply the property will obviously not be habitable and virtually worthless.

You may be told that the property currently gets its water from a neighbour but that the local council are planning to install mains water in the area, or that you can apply to connect to the mains supply yourself. If this is the case then do not take somebody's word for it — go to the local council to check the likely costs involved, as it could be quite expensive.

Also, remember that a neighbour could in the future change his/her mind about supplying you with water, so this needs to be carefully considered.

Council water is metered and the bills are usually sent monthly although some areas may be changing to quarterly or even annual bills. Quite often bills will be estimated and corrected later. Payment can be made by direct debit, via *multibanco* (Portuguese ATM) with a payment reference cited on the bill or in person.

To request to be connected to the mains supply you will usually need to produce the following: ID, fiscal Nº (*número de contribuinte* or *NIF*), *caderneta* and/or deed (*escritura*).

If the property has a well then you would be very wise to see it in the bone dry summer months as well as the wetter winter ones to ensure it doesn't dry up.

If there is a borehole then is it only for your use or shared? When was the borehole pump last maintained and how old is it? What are the likely costs involved in maintaining it?

If there is a water tank, what is its condition like? Is a water quality check advisable?

Rural properties will not be on mains drainage so check that the property has a septic tank *(fossa)* and if not, if it is feasible to install one. If there is already one there, have its condition assessed.

If you buy a property with a borehole then you should check that it has an up-to-date licence. The licence is called an *Alvará de Licença de Captação de Águas*

Subterrânea and needs to be renewed on its expiry, which is currently every 10 years.

Both boreholes and septic tanks, which empty into the water table or soil, are required to be registered with the *ARH (Administração da Região Hidrográfica)* under a law introduced back in May 2007. Springs, rivers, dams, reservoirs, lakes, ponds and wells on property must also be registered under this law. Check that this has been carried out.

Regional offices for the *ARH* can be found by going to *www.apambiente.pt* and clicking on *Instrumentos* on the top bar, followed by *Licenciamento das Utilizações dos Recursos Hídricos* and then *Formulários* on the left-hand side.

If you decide that you would like to buy a property and after purchase dig for a borehole then make sure that you will gain permission for this from the local council *(câmara municipal)* and the *ARH*. You will also need to find out whether there is water of adequate quality on the land. If you are too near the coast, for example, salt water might seep into the supply.

In addition, you will need to check if there are any boreholes within 100m of where you plan to dig as it could interfere with a neighbour's water supply and therefore a licence may not be granted.

It is better to make the enquiries yourself and not leave it to a drilling company, as the client is the responsible party. The application forms (*formulários*) can be found by using the same link as above for the *ARH*.

Get quotations from various drilling companies to compare and make sure that they are licensed to carry out the work.

Some boreholes with a certain engine size and in areas with limited water supply may need to be metered and taxed on usage over a certain amount, so you may also want to check this before purchasing.

If you are buying a ruin on a plot of land which you wish to renovate, and which is without electricity, then check with an electricity company that you will be able to connect and if so, how much it will cost. It could work out quite expensive!

Don't just take a real estate agent's word that you will get electricity quickly and easily. Always check. If a property has never had electricity, it will be a much longer and trickier procedure, as the building must be up to a certain habitable standard to receive permission for a connection to be made. If it is not to the required standard, then work would have to be carried out to make sure that it is.

Check how far the property is from the nearest transformer. Companies will usually be able to connect you if you are less than a kilometre from the nearest one. If not, then you may have to pay for an additional transformer and line, so it is advisable to get a quotation first before proceeding with a purchase.

To request a new connection you will usually need to supply ID, your fiscal Nº (*número de contribuinte* or *NIF*), the *caderneta* and/or deed (*escritura*). The same will need to be produced to change a current supply into your name after purchase.

If the property needs work carried out in order to bring it up to a standard to have an electricity supply, the following will be required: plans of a certified electrician, his installation certificate, habitation licence (*licença de habitação*), property location map and a circuit summary plan (*ficha electrotécnica*).

Until fairly recently, *EDP* (*www.edp.pt*) was the only electricity company in Portugal. However, the market has now been opened up and several other electricity suppliers exist to choose from, for example:

- *www.edp.pt/pt*
- *www.gasnaturalfenosa.pt*
- *www.galpenergia.com/PT*
- *www.endesa.pt*
- *www.iberdrola.pt*

For a full list, go to the *ERSE* (*Entidade Reguladora dos Serviços Energéticos* - regulatory body for energy suppliers in Portugal) website at *www.erse.pt*.

They also have a simulator on their site, which can work out comparisons between the various companies. Once on the site, click on *Simuladores* on the left-hand side and then on *Simulador de Preços de Energia Elétrica – Efetue a sua simulação*.

Although this is only in Portuguese, there is a video showing you what to do. You will need a current electricity invoice for the property to make a comparison.

Bills are usually sent out every two months although you can sometimes request them monthly for a set amount. Meter readings are typically taken about twice a year and are estimated for the rest of the time. However, you may be able to supply your own more accurate readings by telephone, or via the company's website, and have the bills adjusted.

Bills include a fixed charge, plus charges for the amount of electricity used and VAT (*IVA*). There is also a small charge made for TV and radio added to each bill. Reduced economy tariffs, such as *bi-horário* and *tri-horário*, are available on request.

You can pay your electricity bills by direct debit, via *multibanco* (Portuguese ATM) with a payment reference cited on the bill, or in person at the post office (*correios*) or local electricity company office.

Although Portugal has no natural gas resources of its own, mains gas (*gás domicilio*) is available in the bigger cities and towns via imported supplies from places such as Algeria and Nigeria. However, only newer houses and apartments tend to have gas central heating due to the high costs involved in installing it.

Until recently, *Galp Energia* was the only gas provider in Portugal but like electricity this market has now been opened up. Consult the electricity suppliers' links above as well as the *ERSE* website for more information on gas suppliers and distribution.

Billing and payment methods, and applications to be connected will tend to be the same as for electricity.

In areas where there is no mains gas, gas bottles (*garrafas de gás*) are commonly used. The gas is normally butane, but propane is also available. Both can be bought in small quantities. Bottled gas is often used in calor gas-type heaters to heat houses that do not have central heating and also to heat water via an *esquentador* (water heater).

In addition to the cost of the gas, a deposit is usually required for the first bottle bought. From then on, the empty bottle can be exchanged when paying for a full one. You can buy bottles of gas at supermarkets, petrol stations and hardware stores. You can also have gas bottles delivered to your home.

In rural areas, gas is often stored in a large tank (*contentor*) outside the house. Generally, the tank is installed by the gas company and remains their property. A supply contract needs to be signed and you will be charged for a fixed minimum usage of gas per year. Property insurers will need to be informed if you have a gas tank.

Similarly, some apartment blocks and housing estates have communal piped gas from a large storage tank. This is usually propane.

If there is no phone line to the property, check if it will be possible to install one and the likely costs and timescale involved. Nowadays, it is usually fairly quick to get a line installed in an urban area, but if the property is in a more remote, rural location then this could take considerably longer. If more poles are required, it could also end up rather expensive.

The once government owned *Portugal Telecom (PT)* is still the largest company and owns most of the line rentals. However, there are now many more companies offering landlines, including the mobile phone companies. Obtaining a landline can also be in the form of a package inclusive of TV and Internet. Here are some links to companies you may wish to consider:

- *www.telecom.pt*
- *www.worldtelecom.pt*
- *www.artelecom.pt*
- *www.cliente.clix.pt*
- *www.cabovisao.pt*
- *www.meo.pt*
- *www.nos.pt*
- *www.vodafone.pt*

What is available to you will depend on the location of the property and such things as whether there is fibre optics, cable or 4G available, and the distance from masts and exchanges. Do your homework and always check the fine print before signing up to a contract.

Surf around the Internet for the best deals and packages for you and talk to others in the area in which you wish to buy to see what companies are offering the best service. You can also browse forums, particularly expat ones, for information and advice.

Applications will generally have to be made by visiting a local branch of the company and you will need to take along some ID, your fiscal number, bank details and proof of address. Billing is usually monthly and payment methods will be much the same as for the other utilities mentioned above.

In summary, check that all utility bills are paid in full before the final deed signing or you could become liable for any debts. Take readings from the meters and log them so that you can check any bills you later receive.

After purchase, make sure that all the contracts are changed over into your name. If you have agreed with your legal representative to do this on your behalf, as part of their paid duties, then make sure that they carry this task out.

Finally, be prepared for the fact that things may often move more slowly in Portugal and you will need a lot of patience in dealing with some authorities, utilities and businesses. If you are a very impatient person, or get stressed over the slightest thing, then consider very carefully if Portugal is the place for you.

NATIVE'S TIP

Some of the websites in this chapter have an option to view in English. However, if you wish to contact them by email, telephone or letter, and do not speak Portuguese, then arrange for an independent Portuguese speaker to do this on your behalf. If you write in English, it is unlikely that you will receive a reply.

Also, free translators on the Internet are not very accurate and normally only give you a literal translation. These are, therefore, best avoided for translating serious and crucial emails, documents and letters.

Energy Efficiency Certificate

Since January 1st 2009 it has been obligatory for residences in Portugal to have an energy efficiency certificate (*certificado energético da habitação*) for the selling process or for renting. In addition, from December 31st 2013 it became mandatory to mention the energy efficiency classification whenever a property is advertised for sale or rent either privately or via a real estate/renting agent.

A certificate is valid for 10 years and a fine can be imposed for non-compliance. This certificate must be shown to the notary at the time of the final deed signing.

These certificates have to be passed by a technician (*perito qualificado* — *PQ*) recognised by the Energy Agency (*ADENE*). To find technicians qualified to pass these certificates you can consult the agency's website at *www.adene.pt*.

Click on *Bolsa de Peritos Qualificados* on the right-hand side under *Links Rápidos* and then tick the box for a private dwelling (*Certificação de Edifícios de Habitação*). You can then select the region (*Região*), district (*Distrito*) and council area (*Concelho*), followed by *Pesquisar* at the bottom for a list of names in your area.

Clicking on a name will give you all their contact details and a copy of their ID card with photo.

You can also check if someone claiming to be a technician is in fact qualified by entering their registration number (*Nº de Perito*) and/or name (*Nome Completo*), and clicking on *Pesquisar*.

When an energy efficiency certificate is requested, a technician will visit the property and check its location, construction materials, insulation, equipment, for example heating and air-conditioning, and sun exposure. The aim is to improve on insulation, reduce energy costs and protect the environment.

After the checks have been carried out, the technician will calculate the property's thermal efficiency and submit the findings to *ADENE*, who will issue a certificate with a grading. The top grade is A+ and the lowest, G. If you own a property with an A or A+ grading, you may be able to claim some deductions on both rates (*IMI*) and income tax.

Although properties licensed for construction before 2006 must have an energy certificate, no particular grade is required. However, properties licensed for construction after July 4th 2006 must fulfil the standards for a grade B or higher.

Swimming Pool Licences

If you are buying a property with a swimming pool already in existence, make sure that you do some necessary checks. There are a lot of illegal swimming pools in Portugal and you do not want to inherit a substantial fine due to its unauthorised construction.

The swimming pool should appear on the land registry certificate *(certidão de registo predial/teor)*, map and *caderneta*. It will either have been included in the original plans and licensed as part of the final habitation licence or it will have been constructed at a later date and given a separate construction licence *(licença de construção)* and utilisation licence *(licença de utilização)* from the local council *(câmara municipal)*.

If you wish to install a pool after purchase then you should make sure that you will get permission to do so. In urban locations things are usually a little more flexible. However, it is always best to check either directly with the local planning department or with a local architect about any works you wish to carry out to your property in order to be on the safe side.

The architect who prepares the project for the swimming pool will have to check that a pool is allowed in the area in which you wish to build it and that it falls within the rules of the *PDM* (see the *Real Estate Agents & Vendors'* chapter for more on the *PDM*). The project will then be submitted to the local council under what is known as a *comunicação prévia*. They have 30 days to respond.

If they do not respond within the 30-day period then you have tacit approval to go ahead with the building works. However, if the local council has to consult a third party then they are allowed more time.

In rural areas known as *RAN* (agricultural land) or *REN* (ecological land) you will find it extremely difficult, if not impossible, to gain permission for a swimming pool. So check first to avoid disappointment!

Maps

Maps of the property you intend to buy and its boundaries can be found at the local council *(câmara municipal)*.

You will need to know the plot number (usually one or two letters followed by a number, e.g. BQ157) and the parish *(freguesia)* it falls under.

Copies of these maps usually cost just a few Euros and you can purchase maps of varying scales and types.

Some of the local councils, however, have very old maps, which have not been updated for many years.

To obtain more up-to-date maps, go to your regional *Direção-Geral do Território* or order via their website at *www.dgterritorio.pt*. Click on *Contactos* at the top for details of the various regional offices and *Produtos e Serviços* for the various things you can order. They also keep records of ownership and details of the history of the plot, for example if it has been split up or merged with another plot in the past.

Alternatively, you can view maps online by going to *www.dgterritorio.pt* and clicking on *Cadastro* on the top bar and then *Cadastro Geométrico da Propriedade Rústica (CGPR)*, followed by *Consultar secções cadastrais* on the left-hand side. Just enter your district (*Distrito*), council (*Concelho*), parish council (*Freguesia*) and plot section letters (*Secção*) and click on *Seleccionar* to view. You can zoom in and out and move up and down as you need.

CASE STUDY: DONNA & PETER NUTTER

The decision to move to Portugal came when my husband, Pete, and I found that we were spending less and less time together as a family. This was largely due to work and the demands of the transport company Pete owned with his father, which involved long hours and a lot of stress. His parents had been contemplating buying a property abroad in order to spend the winters away and so Pete and I, who also wanted out of the rat race, decided to join them in looking at a move overseas. We also looked at moving to the countryside within the UK.

After looking at various options and countries and not finding exactly what we wanted, Pete's parents came back from their annual holiday in the Algarve. They informed us that property wasn't quite as expensive as they had expected and asked if we fancied giving it a go over there. We started our research and checked on various websites and forums to get background information regarding the possible pitfalls and negatives, as well as the advantages of relocating there.

After this, Pete, his father and uncle went to Portugal for a week and viewed potential properties and businesses. Anyone considering a move to Portugal has to realise that without fluency in the language or a specific qualification and/or an Internet-run business you are limited as to what work you can do. We didn't have the language skills and so, after careful consideration, we opted for a resort/holiday business.

Condominiums

If you buy an apartment, a townhouse or house on a private condominium *(condomínio)* then you will obviously have to pay community fees *(gastos de comunidade)* for the maintenance of communal areas.

These might include such things as:

- ❑ Gardens and grounds
- ❑ Swimming pools
- ❑ Lighting
- ❑ Painting
- ❑ Cleaning
- ❑ Insurance
- ❑ Administration

These charges are calculated on the basis of each owner's share in the development or apartment block, and this percentage should be written in the deed. The shares also determine the voting rights at the annual meeting.

In addition, the condominium will have a set of rules and restrictions. Therefore, it is wise to obtain a copy of these and do some research regarding the management before agreeing to purchase a property on a condominium.

A condominium usually has a paid administrator and by law there has to be an annual general meeting (AGM). This is held before mid-January. At the AGM the administrator must show the expenditure against the budget that was approved for the previous year, set a new budget and seek approval for the administrator for the coming year. If you are unable to attend, you can usually make a proxy vote.

Other meetings may also be called by the administrator or by a group of owners who represent at least 25% of the invested capital.

A registered letter must be sent ten days before the meeting indicating the date, time and place, together with an agenda outlining the subjects to be discussed. A majority is needed to carry any decisions although there may be exceptions where two-thirds or a unanimous decision is required.

At least 50% of owners should be present at the AGM. If 50% are not in attendance, a second meeting date must be called unless it has already been agreed in the notification that it will go ahead at a subsequent meeting with any number of owners present. Sometimes this second meeting will go ahead on this basis on the very same day.

A letter must be sent within 30 days to all those not present advising of the decisions made at the meeting.

Non-residents should supply their permanent address or that of their representative in Portugal to the administrator.

Check that the fees for the property have been paid up to date so that you do not become liable for them after the purchase. It is now mandatory for a vendor to provide this information to a potential buyer, so make sure you ask the question. Owners who do not pay their community fees can have their voting rights removed and have an embargo placed on the property. If they continue unpaid, the property can even be sold at auction.

Also, make sure to check the minutes of annual meetings and previous charges to help determine if any additional charges due to maintenance work are likely, or if the fees are likely to rise substantially. This is especially important in the case of older, more run-down properties.

If possible, speak to other owners already living there to get an idea of the community and how it is run.

By law, condominium companies must have public liability insurance, which should cover anything related to the condominium administration.

There must also be a bank account (which can be a savings or investment account) set up as a reservation fund, in addition to a day-to-day bank account, necessary for maintenance and other works that are required from time to time. It is called a *fundo comum de reserva* and should be at least 10% of the owners' contributions.

The administrator must make any information available regarding this and other bank accounts set up for the condominium on request.

For more information on condominium legislation you can consult a very useful website at *www.gestaodocondominio.pt*. However, it is currently only available in Portuguese. Click on *Administração* and then *Legislação/Propriedade Horizontal* on the left-hand side.

Summary: Top Ten Buying Tips

1. Think very carefully about your reasons for buying a property in Portugal and/or relocating. Do your homework thoroughly, especially if you need to work and/or have children to consider. Take your time and don't rush into things!

2. Rent if possible before relocating permanently, in order to make sure that the area, or even the country, is right for you. Consider renting out your home in your country of origin first before selling up lock, stock and barrel.

3. Choose your own independent and fully qualified legal advice and avoid using the legal representatives put forward by a real estate agent, builder or vendor.

4. Be careful who you use to introduce you to properties and vendors. Check out their credentials and where applicable, their qualifications and any governing body/company registrations.

5. Only use qualified and properly registered builders and architects — preferably recommended from an independent source. View their previous work before engaging them.

6. Do your own property document gathering and checks, alongside any legal help you may choose to use. Get hold of the plans of the building as well as a map of the property and its boundaries, and the area.

7. Do not evade tax or do anything else untoward. This might cost you much more than you saved in the long run!

8. Seek independent financial advice from a reputable and qualified source before parting with any money in Portugal. Let them help you plan properly and thoroughly for your relocation and/or retirement abroad.

9. Learn as much Portuguese as you can and use independent translators for any important document signings, so that you know exactly what you are agreeing to.

10. Do only as you would feel comfortable doing in your home country and don't cut important corners to avoid expense. You may regret it later!

Selling a Property

Although this book is mostly concerned with buying a property in Portugal, I feel it necessary to also make some mention about selling a property.

It is a fact of life that some people may wish to return to where they came from, move to another country, or simply move elsewhere within Portugal at a later stage.

The first thing you need to decide on is whether you are going to use a real estate agent or to sell privately. In addition, you will also need to decide on whom your market is going to be. Will it be native or foreign, or perhaps both?

To sell privately, the simplest thing you can do is to put a for sale (*vende-se*) sign on your property, but be warned, as well as prospective buyers contacting you, so will a number of real estate agents touting for your business.

At this stage, you should also consider how attractive your property looks to potential buyers. Unless you are just selling a ruin for renovation, presentation of your property is obviously of vital importance.

First impressions are crucial, both in relation to the exterior and interior. A property that appears to have been cared for will tend to sell quicker, and often for more, than one that has been neglected and left to fall into disrepair. You should consider seemingly minor things that can make a big difference, such as repairing broken gates and tiles, and cleaning paintwork, shutters and windows. Go round your home with a critical eye, and remove as much junk and clutter as possible to give people a feel for what it might be like if it was their home.

While not spending vast amounts of money that you may never recoup, you many want to consider replacing a few items, such as worn out kitchen units or bathroom suites, to give it more appeal. Simple things like a few flowers dotted around the rooms, soft music, adequate lighting and the smell of freshly brewed coffee may make your home seem more attractive to potential buyers.

After placing a for sale sign on your property, the next step might be to place advertisements in classified sections of newspapers and magazines (UK and/or Portuguese depending on your market) on Internet forums, on free property websites, social media like Facebook and on other existing property websites.

However, note that newspaper and magazine classifieds tend to be very expensive, as do some websites.

If you decide to set up your own website to advertise your property, then you must be sure that you will get enough people viewing it. How are you going to do this? Are you able to design the site or will you have to pay someone else to design it for you?

If this all seems like too much work and hassle then you will need to approach one or several real estate agents. They will usually have expert knowledge of the market, the necessary contacts, an established website and also the marketing know-how that you might lack.

Getting recommendations from others who have sold is also an extremely good idea, as some agents are excellent, while others are a complete waste of time.

Once you have some recommendations then you should check out their credentials and qualifications just as you would for buying. Read the *Real Estate Agents & Vendors'* chapter to refresh your memory on how to go about doing this using the *INCI* website — *www.inci.pt*.

Real estate agents in Portugal charge high commissions, usually between 3% and 6%. Some have even been known to ask for 10%. Negotiate with agents to see if you can get the percentage reduced. However, bear in mind that the more agents you have marketing your property, the less likely they are to agree to a lower percentage.

Some agents request exclusive rights, but tying yourself down to an exclusive deal for a fixed period of time will not enhance your chances of getting a quick sale so it is usually better to have your property on the market with several real estate agents.

It also makes sense to go with agents who advertise in different places and who use different methods including the web in order to give your property a lot more marketing exposure.

Like everything else, a property has a market value and you must ask a realistic price if you wish to get a quick sale.

Listen to your real estate agent's advice and look around at equivalent properties for sale in your area to get a feel for what you should be asking for.

With regard to the agreed asking price, keep a close eye on what your property is being marketed for on agents' websites and portfolios. It is not unheard of for an agent to agree a price with a vendor but then to go away and inflate it substantially in order to get more commission.

Once you have decided on which agents you are going to put your property on the market with, you will be asked to sign a contract known as a *contrato de mediação*. This will state the terms of agreement, whether it is exclusive, details of the property, the price you are seeking, the commission to be paid and when and how it is to be paid. If there is no time period stated, it is considered to be for a six-month duration.

Make sure that you get the Portuguese version of this contract translated into English by an independent translator so that you know exactly what you are agreeing to.

With regard to when the commission is paid, it has been known for some agents to ask for this immediately after they have found you a buyer and the promissory contract has been signed. However, in the unlikely event that the buyer pulls out before the final deed signing, you will be faced with the prospect of having to pay another commission when another buyer for your property is found.

Therefore, it is advisable to pay any commission due after the final deed has been signed and not before. Make sure that this is stated in the *contrato de mediação* and ask the agent for a proper invoice *(factura)* for the commission before handing over any money.

The process and legal requirements for selling a property in Portugal are similar to buying, especially in terms of the documentation.

Your real estate agent has a duty to obtain up-to-date copies of all documentation and to check that all is legitimate and correct before putting your property on the market. The documents usually required are: seller's ID, seller's fiscal Nº, *caderneta predial, certidão de registo predial/teor, licença de habitação* or a pre-1951 certificate, *ficha técnica de habitação*, property plans, the previous *escritura*, borehole licence (if necessary), energy certificate, and if a property is being sold under construction, a *licença de construção* (construction licence). These documents can be found listed in the *What's What* chapter.

You will need to work in conjunction with your agent to make sure that this is carried out. Be certain that you have no outstanding charges, for example rates (*IMI*) against the property or this could delay the sale by many months.

Remember that once you have agreed a price for the sale and signed a promissory contract, any backing out on your part will mean that you have to pay the purchaser double the deposit they have put down.

Also make sure that if a real estate agent is involved in the selling of the property that their name and details appear on the final deed *(escritura)*. This is now required by law, so don't agree to any deal to have their name left off, in order to save them paying tax on the commission. Their commission is also an allowable expense if it is correctly documented in this way.

Any fixtures and fittings you wish to sell in the property must be agreed separately with the purchaser and should not be included in the property price.

Lastly, in relation to the sale there is the issue of capital gains tax *(imposto sobre mais valia)* for any property acquired after the 1st of January 1989.

If you own a home in Portugal, which is your principal residence, then on the sale of that property you must roll the money over onto another property in the EU within 36 months (or up to 24 months before the sale) or face capital gains tax. If you do not roll over the money, then you will pay tax on 50% of the gain made.

The gain will be calculated on the basis of what was declared on your deed *(escritura)* when you purchased and what is declared on the deed when you sell. You should always declare the correct values. Not only is this required by law, but it could also leave you worse off in the long run.

If you sell within five years of purchase then you can offset any improvements you have made to the property by producing the invoices *(facturas)* — hence why it is important to ask for invoices from those who work for you and pay the VAT *(IVA)*. An indexation coefficient is also applied to the purchase price to account for inflation.

You must declare the gain on your next personal income tax declaration (*IRS – Modelo 3 anexo G declaração de rendimentos*) after the sale. After any adjustments 50% of the gain will then be added to any other income you have made during that year and taxed at marginal rates.

Non-resident individuals selling a property face an automatic 28% tax rate on the total gain made. There is no rollover.

Speak to a reputable financial adviser to ascertain what your likely tax burden will be.

Renting

Renting can be seen from two different perspectives:

1. Renting somewhere while you are researching your relocation and looking to buy a property.

2. Renting out a property you own, in order to make some income.

In this chapter I will look at both holiday rentals and long-term rentals. However, before doing so, I would like to offer some words of caution with regard to renting out your property. If the only means of supporting your venture, in terms of paying a mortgage, is to receive regular rental income, then please do some thorough research.

Real estate agents will often advise potential buyers that they will have absolutely no problems in renting out their property after purchase, especially for holiday lets. However, this is getting increasingly hard to do. Many renters are becoming buyers and the holiday rental market is extremely competitive.

This is not only the case within Portugal, but also in Europe and worldwide, as many more holiday destinations are opening up to the public.

If you cannot support your buying venture without renting out your property then think very carefully as to whether you should be doing it in the first place. It could be a big risk!

Long-Term Rental

Long-term rentals are more easily found in cities and bigger towns, although it is possible to find them elsewhere.

The properties will not usually be furnished *(sem móveis)*, unless in resort areas, and utilities are rarely included. Rents will vary considerably, according to the area and the size of the property and the facilities on offer. In cities and large towns rents can be very high in relation to salaries.

The minimum period for commercial rental is currently five years. There are exceptions to this, i.e. for educational or professional reasons and tourism.

A contract can be for one year or sometimes less, but it then becomes a rental agreement rather than a legal rental contract.

If you sign a written legal contract *(contrato de arrendamento)* it should be witnessed and notarised.

If you do not speak good Portuguese then you should get this contract translated by an independent translator so you know exactly what you are agreeing to before signing.

The landlord and tenant must each sign an original copy and a third copy should be given to the local tax office *(serviço das finanças)*. The contract should include:

- ❏ The landlord and tenant's ID details.
- ❏ The identification of the property and its location.
- ❏ The habitation licence *(licença de habitação)* details.
- ❏ The date and duration of the contract.
- ❏ The amount of rent per month.

Other information may also be added to the contract, if agreed between the landlord and the tenant. This might include such things as the state of the building and its contents at the time of rental, who is responsible for any repairs and maintenance, the rules and regulations for the condominium (if applicable) and any other restrictions.

A landlord must also have a basic buildings insurance policy and the tenant should take out his or her own personal contents insurance.

After signing the contract, the tenant then has to pay the first month's rent, plus a deposit, which is usually of the same amount.

Rent increases are allowed as follows:

- • Contracts less than eight years — annually by an amount determined by the government.

- Contracts more than eight years – the means of calculating the annual increase can be specified in the contract.

- As a result of any building works and improvements the landlord is required to make by the local council (*câmara municipal*) the rent can be increased in accordance with the value of the works.

A landlord needs to give the tenant 30 days notice in writing of any increase. A tenant can accept, revoke or query the calculation. Any queries that cannot be resolved between the landlord and tenant may go to a special commission at the local tax office in order for them to make a decision.

A landlord and tenant may agree to terminate a rental contract at any time and this should normally be done in writing. Outside of this, the law specifies different periods of notice for terminating an agreement or contract as follows:

- Over six years – 6 months.

- Between one and six years – 60 days.

- Between three months and one year – 30 days.

- Less than three months – third of the duration.

A tenant can terminate the contract at any time if the landlord does not fulfil their conditions and may also request compensation.

A landlord can request to have a tenant evicted via the courts for the following:

- Failure to pay the rent on time.
- Using the property for activities other than those previously agreed with the landlord, or for carrying out illegal, immoral or dishonest acts.
- Carrying out any building works, which have not been approved by the landlord.
- Sub-letting or lending out of the property, totally or partially, without the landlord's consent.
- Sub-letting the property for a higher rent than that which has been approved by the landlord.
- Leaving the house unoccupied for more than a year.

A landlord can also give notice for the tenant to leave when:

- The house is required for their personal use or for that of their family.
- They are intending to carry out major renovation works for which they are already in possession of a licence from the local authorities.

After having placed a copy of the rental contact with the local tax office, as detailed above, a landlord must then declare his or her rental income in their annual tax return (IRS).

There are a number of tax benefits and allowable expenses of which a landlord can take advantage. A financial adviser will be able to provide advice on this, as well as a landlord's liabilities.

For more information on the law governing long-term renting you can consult the *NRAU* (*Novo Regime do Arrendamento Urbano*) government website at *www.arrendamento.gov.pt/nrau*. It is currently only available in Portuguese.

Holiday Rental

Holiday rentals are for holidaymakers or those who only wish to stay for a few weeks or months. The properties are usually furnished *(mobiliado)* and the rental agreement will normally include the utilities.

In the summer months, particularly in resort areas, these can be very difficult to come by and when they are available the prices tend to be very high. Outside the summer months you will find things a lot easier with many landlords keen to fill the empty autumn and winter months. However, should you begin renting during these off-peak months, be warned that your landlord may not be keen to extend your contract into the summer period.

You will need to sign a rental agreement and if it is a long stay of more than a few weeks then you may be required to pay one month's rent in advance with another month's rent as a deposit.

Short-term rental agreements do not give a tenant the same rights as a long-term contract. If you do not speak good Portuguese, then you should get this document translated by an independent translator before agreeing to sign.

There are three categories for short-term holiday rental properties and these are:

a. Houses – standalone family homes.

b. Apartments – individual, or blocks of apartments.

c. Guest houses – rooms are individual units.

These fall under a term known as *Alojamento Local* and anyone wishing to rent out one of the above types of property will first need to notify the local tax department (*serviço das finanças*) by submitting an *início de actividade* (start of business activity) form and then the local council (*câmara municipal*).

The local council will need to be provided with the following:

❑ Authorization and ID for the person or company making the application to rent the property.

❑ Identification of ownership, including any business name, tax identification number and contact address.

❑ Address of the property being rented.

❑ Capacity of the property: number of bedrooms, beds and users.

❑ Intended start date of the rental activity.

❑ Emergency contact: name, address and telephone number.

- ❏ Confirmation by the applicant of their responsibility for the integrity of the building and for ensuring that it complies with all the legal and regulatory standards.
- ❏ The *caderneta predial* for the property.
- ❏ A copy of the lease/rental agreement.
- ❏ The *início de actividade* form from the tax department.

Properties renting out over nine bedrooms and/or 30 beds are excluded from *Alojamento Local* and will come under the hotel development laws.

Under the category of "guest houses," there is also the classification of "hostel." To be considered a hostel, there must be a minimum of four beds in a room (less if they are bunk beds).

If the person applying has a *Cartão de Cidadão* (Portuguese Citizen's Card), then the whole application process can be made online via the *Portal da Empresa* website at *www.portaldaempresa.pt*.

Click on *Empresa Online* and then *Balcão do Empreendedor* and go to *Turismo* in the list, followed by *Alojamento*. In the next list that appears, click on *Alojamento em moradia ou apartamento* and finally, *Alojamento local – registo da actividade* where you will see *Obter formulário* (to obtain form) and *Realizar serviço* (to carry out the service) halfway down.

For those without a *Cartão de Cidadão*, you can still print out the form using this website and then fill it in and take it to your nearest local council (along with the information and documentation previously listed) where you will be issued with a registration number.

The local council will usually carry out an inspection within 30 days of submitting the notification to make sure that the property complies with health and safety, and hygiene standards and regulations. They can also request a visit from the Portuguese tourist board (*Turismo de Portugal*) at any time. The council may make a charge for the inspection.

A plate (200mm x 200mm) with the initials *AL* (*Alojamento Local*) now only needs be displayed outside the principal entrance of a rental accommodation classified as a "guest house" or "hostel."

In any advertising and documentation, the registration number issued by the local council should be displayed.

A holiday rental property must conform to the following:

- ❏ Have fire safety equipment, e.g. a fire extinguisher and fire blanket, a first-aid box, instruction manuals for appliances and emergency telephone numbers.
- ❏ Be in good general condition, both inside and out, furnished to a decent standard and have good standards of cleanliness and hygiene.
- ❏ Be connected to the mains sewerage system or have a septic tank *(fossa)*.

- ❏ Be connected to the water mains or have a private, licensed water supply with clean running hot and cold water.
- ❏ Each room must have a window to the outside for ventilation and a means to block outside light.
- ❏ Locks on the doors, both for security and privacy.
- ❏ Bed linen and towels should be changed at least once a week and whenever there is a client changeover.
- ❏ A minimum of one bathroom for every three bedrooms; each containing a toilet, washbasin and bath or shower.
- ❏ Rules and regulations of the property and condominium displayed (where applicable), and general information on services provided, etc.
- ❏ Have a complaints book *(livro de reclamações)*.

CASE STUDY: DAVID HINMAN

An expat with a difference: *Olá*, I'm David, I'm English, and my wife Isabel is Portuguese. We met and married in London in the late 1980s, when both in our 30s. For more than a decade we visited Portugal once or twice a year and constantly dreamed of retiring there one day. Those were fantastic holidays, and we did — for a few years in the mid-1990s — own a small holiday apartment in the Algarve, but sold it in order to invest in a bigger home in London. In 2001, I found myself out of a job and our dream of retiring to Portugal became reality.

Both in our late 40s at that time, we sold our London home, car and everything that wouldn't fit in the back of the removal van, and started a new life in Lisbon. Although Isabel has family in Lisbon — a lovely, kind and helpful sister — we found getting ourselves organised with a new home, car, GP, permits, licences and all that red tape rather more time-consuming and frustrating than we had imagined. For Isabel, being Portuguese didn't mean a lot when it came to making sense of the system as she had spent most of her adult life in London. However, I do believe the fact she is Portuguese meant we got more than our fair share of nods and winks from property developers, agents, lawyers and accountants. One must remember that Portugal has an unfortunate modern history, as for nearly half a century — up until the revolution of 1974 — its people lived under a corrupt regime. Following the revolution, everyone wanted a share in this corrupt way of life. The EEC rescued the country in 1986, but old habits die hard.

Within about six months of moving to Portugal, we had bought two brand-new apartments in Lisbon: one to rent out and one to live in. The rental was long-term, which means that under Portuguese law the tenant has the right to stay for up to five years. This means that it's not only a potentially long-term commitment for you, the landlord, but also that you should charge a high rent from the outset as you are allowed to increase it annually by no more than the rate of inflation (officially 3% or 4% but in reality something higher).

Our first tenant moved out after nearly two years and we decided to sell that property and buy one in a new development on the Cascais coast for us to live in. After moving to Cascais, we had a tenant in our Lisbon property for another couple of years. This long-term renting was working out well for us and we were attracting foreign businessmen through letting agents with a dot.com presence.

In 2006, after nearly five years of Portuguese life and just the two long-term rental experiences, we had some serious thought about our future. Did we really want to spend the rest of our lives there? We were making enough to live quite comfortably, but saving hardly a cent. Both our properties were of the sought-after kind but were not increasing in value half as fast as London property might. Neither of us had found a proper job and I was struggling with the language. I had a blood disorder, which was having no effect on me at that time, but would have led to something serious without proper diagnosis and treatment, which is simply unavailable on the Portuguese NHS and almost certainly unavailable at any Portuguese private hospital too. Isabel is proud to be Portuguese (all Portuguese are!), loves being in Portugal and plans to spend many a future holiday on Portugal's beaches, but she confesses to favour life in England. So we sold up and moved back.

We had a wonderful five years in Portugal and have absolutely no regrets. We are now back in London as happier and spiritually healthier beings. The whole exercise didn't make sense financially as we've had to go down the London property ladder, but hey, we lived in the sun doing nothing for five years.

My advice to anyone thinking of moving to Portugal:
You must go with every intention of staying and making a success of it, but if you do return, you have not failed. If anyone's failed, it was he who never tried.

Don't burn your bridges in the UK — things like keeping a bank account open will make life a whole lot simpler if you do go back, and you may consider things like paying voluntary national insurance contributions (if that is still allowed) beneficial.

The proverbial grass is no greener. It just looks, feels and tastes different. *Boa sorte!*

David Hinman, London (previously Lisbon)

Residency

In 2006 Portugal came in line with other EU countries and implemented the EU Directive 2004/58/EC. Therefore, immigration for EU citizens should be fairly straightforward. However, for non-EU citizens other rules will apply.

Note that citizens of Iceland, Norway, Liechtenstein, Andorra and Switzerland can also apply under the same rules as EU citizens.

Visits

For visits of up to three months only a passport is required.

Residency Certificate

After three months, and within 30 days, you must then apply for a residency certificate (*Certificado de Registo*) at your local council *(câmara municipal)*. According to most councils, the only documentation that is required is a passport or national ID card and your Portuguese fiscal Nº, obtained from the local *Serviço das Finanças* (see the *Tax Office — Serviço das Finanças* section of the *What's What* chapter). You simply have to make a self-declaration regarding whether you are employed, self-employed or have other means to live, whether you have health insurance (if not entitled to the Portuguese health system) and other details regarding your education and family.

However, it may be best to call ahead to check with your particular local council as to which documents they need, as some also seem to request the European health card, as well as proof of address and income.

You will then be issued with an A4 paper certificate, which is valid for five years. This does not mean that you have to give up residency in your own country (you are legally entitled to be resident in two EU countries at the same time). You should carry this document with you at all times and inform the local council if you are no longer residing in Portugal.

Residency Card

If you are still residing in Portugal after five years and wish to continue to do so, you must apply within 30 days for a residency card (*Cartão de Residência Permanente*) at your nearest immigration office (*Serviço de Estrangeiros e Fronteiras – SEF*). The documents required are a passport or national ID card, two passport-type photos and your previous residency certificate. In addition, you may be asked for your last tax (*IRS*) return and other documents, so it may be best to call ahead first to double check with the *SEF* in your area. Fingers prints are also taken.

You will then be issued with a small plastic card with a photo. It must be renewed every ten years, but this is merely a formality to update your photo and refresh the document. The expiry date will be listed on the card.

Once you have a permanent residency card, you should inform the *SEF*, as well as the local tax office, if you permanently leave Portugal, and as for the previous certificate, you should always have it on your possession.

At the time of writing, both the residency certificate and card, and card renewals cost €15 on application.

Immigration Office — Serviço de Estrangeiros e Fronteiras (SEF)

The immigration office (*Serviço de Estrangeiros e Fronteiras — SEF*) have a website at *www.sef.pt*.

You can use this site not only for up-to-date residency and immigration information, but also to make an appointment online to renew your residency at the nearest *SEF*. Click next to the British flag in the top left-hand corner if you need to view in English and then on *Online appointment in a SEF Delegation* in the box on the right-hand side of the page.

Alternatively, you can telephone the *SEF* on 808 202 653 from a landline or 808 962 690 from a mobile. You can then select option one for an appointment or option two for further information. The service is available in various languages, including English, French, Russian, Ukrainian and Romanian.

Some *SEF's* are also now able to take your photos, but make sure that you check before you go that your nearest office has this facility available. If not, you will still have to take along your own photos as before.

Non-EU Citizens

For non-EU citizens you should consult your particular embassy or Portuguese consulate in your home country for details of your entry and visa requirements, as these can differ from country to country.

To gain entry to Portugal you will need at least a passport (valid for more than three months after the intended period of stay), an entry visa and proof of means of subsistence for the duration of the stay and to return home.

There are several different types of visa, such as short-stay, transit, residence, study and work. If you intend to live in Portugal, then it is advisable to obtain a residence visa.

Once you have an entry visa you can then consult the nearest *SEF* for further immigration information and requirements, which will often include (amongst other things) a criminal background check.

An electronic residency card has now been introduced for non-EU citizens, which is similar to the Portuguese citizens' all-in-one, 'super' ID card. It has a chip that not only stores residency information, but also fiscal and social security details. Renewals of this card can be dealt with as per the information supplied above for EU citizens, i.e. the online appointment system or by telephone.

Documents required for this card include a valid passport, fiscal N°, proof of address and income, and two passport-type photos. However, as previously mentioned, it is always best to check with the office that you will be attending as to the documents required, in order not to have a wasted trip.

Golden Visa

In October 2012 a scheme was launched in Portugal called the "Golden Visa" (*Visto de Ouro*). This is a fast track system for non-EU foreign investors whereby they can obtain a residency permit in Portugal and are able to travel freely within those countries signed up to the Schengen agreement.

The aim is to attract increased foreign investment in Portugal.

The following types of investment qualify:

   i.   The transfer of capital with a value equal to or above one million Euros.

   ii. The creation of at least ten jobs.

iii.   The acquisition of real estate with a value equal to or above 500, 000 Euros.

The Golden Visa can be applied for at Portuguese Diplomatic or Consular Posts or at a regional *SEF*. The application can also be carried out online via the *SEF* website.

For more information and to apply online, go to *www.sef.pt* and click on the box in the middle of the page called *Golden Residence Permit Programme*.

Tax

It is beyond the scope of this book to go into great detail about personal taxation, but it should nevertheless be noted that there is a difference between physical residency and fiscal residency.

Whereas you need to apply for a residency certificate after being in Portugal for three months, you become a tax resident only if you stay more than 183 days a year in Portugal, either continuously or interrupted, or if you stay less than 183 days but have a permanent place of residence established by the year end.

Whereas permanent, fiscal residents are taxed on their worldwide income (at various rates depending on the income bracket), non-residents will only pay tax on their earned income inside Portugal. This will usually be at a 25% flat tax rate. Portugal has signed treaties with many countries in order to avoid double taxation, so you should receive a tax credit in your home country to avoid paying twice. You must declare your income in the country where it is generated.

You can also obtain a certificate of fiscal residency online in order to prove your tax residency in Portugal to other countries to avoid double taxation. Go to the *Portal das Finanças website* at *www.portaldasfinancas.gov.pt* and click on the box called *Serviços Tributários*. Once you have signed in via the *O Seu Espaço* section on the right, click on *Serviços Tributários* on the left-hand side and then *Obter*, followed by *Consultar Certidões*. In the *Certidão* box click on the arrow and highlight *Residência Fiscal*, and then enter the dates you request (*Data do Pedido*). Finally, click on *Continuar* at the bottom. See the *Tax Office — Serviço das Finanças* section of the *What's What* chapter to find out about how to create an account. To log out, click on *fechar sessão*.

If you are a tax resident in two countries at the same time then this will be resolved under the international tax treaties' rules.

In 2009 Portugal introduced the Non-Habitual Resident regime. Under this regime, you only pay a 20% flat rate on income (employed or self-employed) and are exempt from paying tax on foreign sourced income, such as pensions, renting, capital gains, interest, etc, as long as certain conditions are met. These relate to whether the income is (or could be) taxed in the source country.

This is of particular benefit to those who work in "high value added" activities, such as actors, architects, artists, company directors, dentists, doctors, engineers, musicians, professors, etc, as the top rate of tax is currently 48%.

To qualify for this you must not have been a resident in Portugal in the previous five tax years and need to register with the tax office *(serviço das finanças)* as a new tax resident. The benefits last for ten years as long as you continue to meet Portugal's tax residency requirements.

Renting out a furnished property on a short-term basis to tourists usually comes under a special category of taxation whereby only 15% of the income earned is taxed, the balance being exempt to cover business overheads.

Taxation is a very complex and personal subject and so it is advisable to obtain expert tax advice before relocating to Portugal. This advice should preferably be from someone knowledgeable in both Portuguese taxation and the taxation system in your current country of residence.

You should advise the tax authorities upon leaving your home country permanently — you might even be due for a refund.

On arriving in Portugal and starting work, or a business, you should inform the tax office *(serviço das finanças)* as soon as possible. Portugal has a PAYE system of income tax, whereby an employee's tax is held at source and the self-employed must adhere to a personal system of declaration.

Tax (*IRS*) declarations can be made by paper or online at the *Portal das Finanças* website, once you have signed in. The return is known as a *Modelo 3*. There are different dates for submission depending on whether it is done online or paper and according to the type of income. Check either the *Portal das Finanças* website for the date, or with a professional financial adviser or accountant.

Traditionally a tax evader's paradise, Portugal is now beginning to get to grips with those who try to avoid paying — particularly foreigners. So be warned! Seek good advice rather than risk getting caught. You will not only have to pay back the tax owed, but may also suffer heavy fines, or worse get permanently 'blacklisted'.

CASE STUDY: BEN TAYLOR

My wife, Louise, and I spent several years planning our move to Portugal. We are perhaps not your typical migrants to the country, both being in our mid-thirties.

We were doing perfectly well in London. My wife had a well-paid job and I had built up a successful, though maddeningly stressful, IT business. We lived in a good area of London, drove a nice, shiny car and had money in the bank.

Due to my overwhelming need to constantly chase the sunshine, we took plenty of short holidays, usually to Portugal (once we discovered the country we didn't really want to go anywhere else). Sadly, calls from frantic clients and the constant vibration of my smartphone invariably interrupted these breaks.

One day, we were on holiday on the beautiful Portuguese island of Porto Santo, off the coast of Madeira. It was about 5 P.M., and as I sat on my lounger I looked out to the sea and saw a local man sitting on the edge of the shore with his young son. They looked so content.

At that moment I had a terrifying vision of the future! Our lives in London were on a stereotypical path, and I knew exactly what was five years further down it: a bigger house in a slightly more affluent area of London, a bigger, shinier car and a bit more money in the bank. Alongside these things would be longer hours, a phone that vibrated ever more frequently and, worst of all, children who would have closer relationships with their nanny than with us.

I had seen so many lives like this and I didn't want any part of it. I wanted to be that Portuguese man sitting on the shore with his son.

We spent the next three years planning and researching. My wife was very fortunate to have a progressive employer, who accepted that she could perform her role from a distance, making full use of technologies such as Skype. That was the first *major* hurdle jumped — it is difficult to find well-paid employment in Portugal, even with fluent Portuguese.

I put a plan in place to trim down my business and diversify into web-based work that I, too, could do from a distance — all with the emphasis on not taking my stressful life to Portugal with me!

After these years of getting everything in order, building up an emergency fund, and frantically 'ebaying' and 'car booting' our vast amount of clutter, the day finally arrived for our move. We bid sad farewells to our friends, some of whom I suspect thought we were crazy to turn our backs on London.

Well, it's fair to say we've proved them wrong, as at the time of writing we've now been in Portugal for nearly five years. Our lives have changed immeasurably since we got here. My wife has been through a redundancy and set up a consultancy of her own; my working life is mostly spent writing; we've published a book; and (most significantly) we've welcomed our first child into the world!

How have we found the Portugal experience so far? In the main it has lived up to our expectations, but it has also been a little more stressful than we had expected. Everyone tells you the bureaucracy is a nightmare — it truly is. When we visit government buildings we treat every tiny bit of progress we make as a step forward; expecting anything to happen quickly in Portugal is the path to disappointment! Also, when you're of working age you do still need to make a living, so our work/life balance hasn't adjusted quite as much as we might have hoped.

What are the plus points? Squeezing in a quick swim or walk on the beach during a working day, having barbecues in the evenings, all year round, and still finding beautiful new sights most weekends. We dreamed about all of these things during the three years of planning — and they have all come true! We remain in love with Portuguese food and with the plentiful markets selling fresh, local produce, which tastes so much better than anything you can buy in an English supermarket. However, with a baby in tow nowadays, we should admit that convenience does now win out more often than not!

What advice would we give people planning to move here? Most importantly, do as much as you can to learn Portuguese — every extra word makes your life easier. Secondly, try to slow down your pace — don't expect anything to happen quickly, and realise that while doubts do come creeping up on you in the early days, they will diminish. Most importantly, eat some sardines, drink that delicious, cheap wine, and enjoy the sunshine!

Ben Taylor, Conceição de Tavira

www.movingtoportugal.org
www.foodandwineportugal.com

About Gabrielle

 A Londoner by birth, I later moved out to Surrey where I attended Nonsuch High School for Girls in Cheam. Being a rather free-spirited person and finding the constraints and curriculum of an all girls' grammar school a bit too much, I left at 16 (to the probable consternation of my headmistress) and started an apprenticeship in structural engineering in London.

However, after not developing much of a passion for designing oil rigs, I decided to return to academic life and obtained both a BA (Hons) in Sports Studies and History and an MSc in Sports Science. During this time I also became a top-class runner, gaining an Athletics National Championship (AAA) medal in the 3000m and various vests for road, cross-country and track. As well as pursuing athletics, I spent time as a part-time teacher and coach, and worked in a specialist running shop.

After having surgery on a calcaneal bursitis and cyst, I decided to retire from running and travelled about for a while, including spending long periods of time in Portugal where my parents were living.

Having already studied French and Spanish at school, and dabbled with Italian, I soon picked up a working knowledge of Portuguese and began to get involved in helping non-Portuguese-speaking expatriates with bureaucracy and property purchase problems. It therefore seemed the logical next step to write a book in order to pass on the knowledge that I had gained in this area, and I was lucky enough to get two editions of *Buying Property in Portugal* published.

This is my third edition and I have tried to make it even more informative than the previous two. Not an easy task when things change so often in Portugal and when there are different local interpretations of regulations.

As well as this title, I have recently released *British Marathon Running Legends of the 1980s*, a project that was originally the basis for my MSc dissertation, and which was kindly sponsored by Sir Eddie Kulukundis. I have also helped Life Coach & NLP Master Practitioner, Midgie Thompson, publish her first book, *Winning Strategies for Sports & Life*.

When I am not writing, I can usually be found in the gym lifting weights and performing a variety of cardiovascular exercise, bodyweight exercises and circuit training. For relaxation, I enjoy nothing more than drinking wine with good friends and going to the odd rock or metal gig. You can read more about me at *www.gabriellecollison.com*.

Appendices

IMT (Purchase Tax) 2015

The tables below show the different scales of purchase tax (*imposto municipal sobre transmissões onerosas de imóveis — IMT*) for urban property as of 2015. Non-permanent occupation refers to holiday homes and second homes as opposed to permanent occupation, which refers to your primary place of residence.

Permanent Occupation	Rate	Deduction
Up to €92,407	0%	€0
€92,407 — €126,403	2%	€1,848.14
€126,403 — €172,348	5%	€5,640.23
€172,348 — €287,213	7%	€9,087.19
€287,213 — €574,323	8%	€11,959.32
> €574,323	6%	€0
Non-Permanent Occupation	**Rate**	**Deduction**
Up to €92,407	1%	€0
€92,407 — €126,403€	2%	€924.07
€126,403 — €172,348	5%	€4,716.16
€172,348 — €287,213	7%	€8,163.12
€287,213 — €550,836	8%	€11,035.25
> €550,836	6%	€0

The following applies for other types of property:

- A building plot or land to build an urban property - 6.5% flat rate.

- A rustic property and agricultural land - 5.0% flat rate.

- A property acquired by a company domiciled in a 'whitelisted' jurisdiction - same rates as those in the table above.

- A property acquired by a company domiciled in a 'blacklisted' jurisdiction - 15% flat rate.

- The purchase of shares of a company in a 'whitelisted' jurisdiction - no *IMT*.

- The purchase of shares of a company in a 'blacklisted' jurisdiction - 8% flat rate.

*Note: In September 2013 a new law was introduced which provides for the gradual abolition of *IMT* between 2016 and 2018. Beginning in 2016, *IMT* rates will be reduced by a third and in 2017, by a further third. *IMT* will only be payable until the 31st of December 2017.

However, in order to comply with European legislation, which states that all real estate transactions must be taxed, it is expected that the Portuguese government will introduce a new tax at this stage.

Property Purchase Checklist

(Make a copy for each property you view.
Remember to take photos, video & GPS coordinates.)

This property purchase checklist should be used in conjunction with your legal representative's checks.

Notes	Property

	Property
	• Price
	• Bedrooms
	• Bathrooms
	• Total Nº Of Rooms
	• Covered Area (m2)
	• Uncovered Area (logradouro/ envelope & land m2)
	• Electricity
	• Water
	    a) Mains
	    b) Borehole
	    c) Well
	    d) Cisterna/Water Tank
	      i. Neighbours Supply
	      ii. Bombeiros Supply
	• Gas
	• Mains Drainage
	• Septic Tank
	• Swimming Pool
	• Garage
	• Phone
	• Internet

Notes

Location
- Countryside
- Village
- Coast
- Town/City

Access
- Poor
- Fair
- Good

Transport
- Roads/Motorways
- Trains
- Buses
- Airport

Amenities
- Medical
  - a) Hospital
  - b) Health Centre/Drs.
- Schools/Colleges
- Entertainment
- Restaurants/Cafés
- Leisure/Sport

Reason
- Investment
- Rental
- Holidays
- For Family
- To Live

Notes

Type
- Plot To Build
- Ruin To Renovate
- New Build
- Off-Plan
- Resale

Type of Land
- Urban
- Rustic
- Agricultural
- Ecological
- Mixed %s

In Working Order
- Boiler
- Heating/Air-Conditioning System
- Water Heating System
- Electrics
- Fitted Appliances
- Borehole Pump
- Cisterna/Water Tank
- Well
- Water Quality
- Septic Tank
- Phone Line
- Internet
- Swimming Pool Equipment
- Irrigation System

Notes

Further Checks

- Rights Of Way
- Adjoining Neighbours Been Asked
- Boundaries Clearly Marked
- Property Map Checked
- Survey Of Boundaries Required
- Survey Of Property Required
- View Likely To Remain
- PDM Checked
- Building/Planning Permission Obtained For All Works Planned
- Builder's Warranty
- Building(s) All Legal
- Swimming Pool Legal
- Borehole Legal
- Condominium Charges Up To Date
- Condominium Rules & Regulations
- All Utility Bills & IMI (council tax) Up To Date

Current Document Checks

- Certidão de Teor/Registo Predial
- Caderneta(s)
- Property Map & Building Plans
- Current Escritura
- Habitation Licence or Pre-1951 Certificate
- Ficha Técnica de Habitação
- Swimming Pool Construction & Utilisation Licences

Notes	• Borehole Licence
	• Borehole & Septic Tank Registered
	• Energy Efficiency Certificate

Check Credentials
- Real Estate Agent's AMI Nº
- UK Company's Registered Nº
- Private Vendor
- Builder's Alvará Nº & Company Nº
- Lawyer or Solicitador's Cédula Nº

Purchase Budget Calculator

(Make a copy & fill it in.)

Property Price _____

IMT Purchase Tax (see 2015 IMT table) _____

IVA (VAT 23,25% - new properties only) _____

Legal Fees (1 to 2% of property value) _____

Notary Fees* _____

Deed Registration Fees* _____

Stamp Duty (0.8%) _____

Survey If Carried Out _____

* Together approx. 1 to 2% of property value

Remember that you will also have to budget for IMI (council tax), and condominium and mortgage fees (where applicable), as well as your everyday maintenance and running costs.